CPAG'S

Housing Benefit and

Council Tax Benefit

Legislation

27th Edition

2014/2015

Supplement

Commentary by

Carolyn George MA

Richard Poynter BCL, MA(Oxon), District Tribunal Judge, Judge of the Upper Tribunal

Stewart Wright MA, Dip. Law, Barrister, Judge of the Upper Tribunal

Martin Williams Welfare rights worker, CPAG

Susan Mitchell Freelance writer on welfare rights

*Statutory instruments up to date to **26 May 2015***

Published by CPAG, 30 Micawber Street, London N1 7TB

CPAG promotes action for the prevention and relief of poverty among children and families with children. To achieve this, CPAG aims to raise awareness of the causes, extent, nature and impact of poverty, and strategies for its eradication and prevention; bring about positive policy changes for families with children in poverty; and enable those eligible for income maintenance to have access to their full entitlement. If you are not already supporting us, please consider making a donation, or ask for details of our membership schemes, training courses and publications.

Published by Child Poverty Action Group
30 Micawber Street, London N1 7TB
Tel: 020 7837 7979
staff@cpag.org.uk
www.cpag.org.uk

© Child Poverty Action Group 2015

This book is sold subject to the condition that it shall not, by way of trade or otherwise, be lent, resold, hired out or otherwise circulated without the publisher's prior consent in any form of binding or cover other than that in which it is published and without a similar condition including this condition being imposed on the subsequent purchaser.
A CIP record for this book is available from the British Library

Main work: ISBN 978 1 906076 87 0

Supplement: ISBN 978 1 906076 88 7

Child Poverty Action Group is a charity registered in England and Wales (registration number 294841) and in Scotland (registration number SC039339), and is a company limited by guarantee, registered in England (registration number 1993854). VAT number: 690 808117

Design by Devious Designs
Content management system by Konnect Soft www.konnectsoft.com
Typeset by David Lewis XML Associates Limited
Printed in the UK by Group (UK) Ltd, Croydon, CR0 4YY

Contents

Introduction

This Supplement to the 27th edition provides commentary on all relevant new caselaw and updates to the legislation to 26 May 2015.

Thanks to Nicola Johnston for editing and managing the production of this book and to Mike Hatt at David Lewis XML.

Comments on this Supplement and the main work are always welcomed and can be sent to the authors via CPAG.

Carolyn George, Richard Poynter, Stewart Wright, Martin Williams and Susan Mitchell

Table of cases

Table of Upper Tribunal and Commmissioners' decisions

How to use this supplement

Use the Noter-up to find out about changes to the main volume. The page numbers on the left refer to pages in the main volume. The entry opposite either states what the change is or refers to another part of this supplement where the amending legislation is set out.

For abbreviations, see pxlii of the main volume.

PART I:

NOTER-UP

General Note

The HB amounts for, for example, personal allowances, premiums, components, non-dependant deductions and deductions from rent are confirmed/uprated by the Social Security Benefits Up-rating Order 2015 SI No.547 and the Welfare Benefits Up-rating Order 2015 SI No.30 as from 1 April 2015 (6 April 2015 if rent is payable weekly or in multiples of a week).

Welfare Reform Act 2012

A number of new commencement orders for provisions for claims and awards of universal credit, and orders amending previous commencements orders (including amendments to the Gateway Conditions for some claimants), have been made. See p1695 of the main volume for a list of the commencements orders made at the time it was written. The new orders and amending orders are as follows.

From 24 November 2014: The Welfare Reform Act 2012 (Commencement No.9, 11, 13, 14, 16, 17 and 19 and Transitional and Transitory Provisions (Amendment)) Order 2014 SI No.3067.

For claims made on or after 24 November but before 20 December 2014: The Welfare Reform Act 2012 (Commencement No.20 and Transitional and Transitory Provisions and Commencement No.9 and Transitional and Transitory Provisions (Amendment)) Order 2014 SI No.3094. Transitional provision is made for claims for HB by art 6 of the order (see p34).

From 26 January, 2 March and 6 April 2015: The Welfare Reform Act 2012 (Commencement No.9, 11, 13, 14, 16, 17 and 19 and Transitional and Transitory Provisions (Amendment)) Order 2015 SI No.32.

From 28 January 2015: The Welfare Reform Act 2012 (Commencement No.21 and Transitional and Transitory Provisions) Order 2015 SI No.33. Transitional provision is made for claims for HB by Article 6 of the order (see p56).

From 16 and 23 February; 2, 9, 16 and 23 March; 6, 13, 20 and 27 April; 4, 11, 18 and 25 May; 1, 8, 18, 22 and 29 June; 6, 13 and 20 July 2015: The Welfare Reform Act 2012 (Commencement No.22 and Transitional and Transitory Provisions) Order 2015 SI No.101.

From 18 March, 10 June and 4 November 2015: The Welfare Reform Act 2012 (Commencement No.23 and Transitional and Transitory Provisions) Order 2015 SI No.634. Transitional provision is made for claims for HB by art 7 of the order (see p78).

pp12-13   SSCBA 1992 s137 – Interpretation of Part VII and supplementary provisions

In Scotland, the definition of "couple" substituted and para (1A) omitted by Sch 4 para 2 of the Marriage and Civil Partnership (Scotland) Act 2014 and Civil Partnership Act 2004 (Consequential Provisions and Modifications) Order 2014 SI No.3229 as from 16 December 2014.

pp37-40   SSAA 1992 s75 – Overpayments of Housing Benefit

[p38: Under the General Note, add as a new penultimate paragraph (ie, before the paragraph beginning "Guidance has been issued…")]

In refusing permission to appeal in *KP v Royal Borough of Kensington and Chelsea* [2014] UKUT 393 (AAC), Judge Wikeley ruled that a criminal court's imposition of a compensation order under the Powers of Criminal Courts (Sentencing) Act 2000 did not act to cap the maximum amount of HB that a local authority can recover under s75 SSAA 1992, and so nothing in the compensation order acted to prohibit the local authority from seeking to recover the balance of the overpayment under s75. In so doing, Judge Wikeley followed *CSB 392/1985* and *CIS 683/1994*.

pp57-8   SSAA 1992 s115A – Penalty as an alternative to prosecution

The amount in s115A(3)(b) increased by art 2 of the Social Security (Penalty as Alternative to Prosecution) (Maximum Amount) Order 2015 SI No.202 as from 1 April 2015, but only in relation to an act or omission referred to in s115A(1)(a) SSAA 1992 which occurred wholly on or after that date.

pp148-49   CSPSSA 2000 Sch 7 para 7 – Redetermination etc of appeals by tribunal

[p148: In the Analysis of para 7(3), at the end of the first sentence, delete the full stop and add:]

see (in the context of the equivalent rule in s13(3) Social Security Act 1998) *GA v SSWP (ESA)* [2014] UKUT 521 (AAC) at para 4.

p180   Tribunals, Courts and Enforcement Act 2007 s12 – Proceedings on appeal to Upper Tribunal

[p180: In the General Note, at the end of the penultimate paragraph, add:]

The Fisrt-tier Tribunal is required to comply with any directions given by the Upper Tribunal when remitting the case: see *SD v SSWP (ESA)* [2015] UKUT 116 (AAC) at para 9.

pp214-35   HB Regs reg 2 – Interpretation

In Scotland, definition of "couple" substituted by Sch 6 para 27 of the Marriage and Civil Partnership (Scotland) Act 2014 and Civil Partnership Act 2004 (Consequential Provisions and Modifications) Order 2014 SI No.3229 as from 16 December 2014.

Definition of "shared parental leave" inserted by art 17(2)(c) of the Shared Parental Leave and Statutory Shared Parental Pay (Consequential Amendments to Subordinate Legislation) Order 2014 SI No.3255 as from 31 December 2014.

Definition of "paternity leave" amended by art 17(2)(a) and (b) of that order as from 5 April 2015. Note: transitional provision is made under art 35.

Para (5)(ab) inserted and para (5)(b) amended by reg 2(2) of the Social Security (Miscellaneous Amendments) Regulations 2015 SI No.67 as from 23 February 2015.

Definition of "training allowance" amended by art 2 and Sch 3 para 8(2) of the Deregulation Act 2015 (Consequential Amendments) Order 2015 SI No.971 as from 26 May 2015.

[p233: At the end of the Analysis of the definition of "shared ownership tenancy", add:]

Judge Mesher considered whether the definition of shared ownership tenancy could apply to a claimant who had acquired the long tenancy of a dwelling under the right to buy legislation: *Blackburn with Darwen Borough Council v DA (HB)* [2014] UKUT 431 (AAC). He concluded that para (a) of the definition had to be qualified by reading in some element of shared ownership, with "ownership" here given its everyday meaning. He said:

> "A shared ownership tenancy is one in which the tenant, in the case of a flat, takes a long-term leasehold interest in only part of the dwelling concerned (typically, 25%, 50% or 75%), while paying rent as a short-term tenant would on the remainder. The tenant then has the right to buy additional percentages on the long-term basis, when amount of the short-term rent will reduce proportionately. The essence is that there is a sharing of what would in ordinary language be regarded as the ownership of the dwelling, between the tenant in the case of the long-term tenancy element and the landlord in the case of the short-term tenancy aspect. The claimant here did not share the ownership of his flat in that sense, and neither would anyone else who acquired a long tenancy of the dwelling as a whole under the right to buy legislation. His ownership under the 125 lease was not shared with the landlord in that sense, even though there was still a split between the freehold interest of the landlord and his leasehold interest. Therefore, the ordinary application of regulation 12(2)(a) of the 2006 Regulations to long tenancies was not excluded in the claimant's case. That conclusion is in my view confirmed by the terms of head (b) of the definition of "shared ownership tenancy" applying to Scotland. There would be no rational reason for applying a different practical policy to the scope of the application of regulation 12(2)(a) as between Scotland and England and Wales."

[p234: In the Analysis to para (3), after the first sentence, add:]

For the meaning of "payable", see the discussion of *SMcH v Perth and Kinross Council (HB)* [2015] UKUT 126 (AAC) in the Analysis of para (3A) below.

[p234: In the Analysis to para (3A), delete the first sentence and add:]

Someone is considered to be on income-related ESA on any day in respect of which it is payable to her/him. In *SMcH v Perth and Kinross Council (HB)* [2015] UKUT 126 (AAC), Judge Mesher decided that "payable" here does not mean "actually paid" or "actually paid under an award whether right or wrong". It means "properly or lawfully paid" or something akin to that. A consequence is that the disregard of income in Sch 5 para 4 HB Regs cannot be triggered by payments of income-related ESA subsequently found to have been made in error – eg, if there was no entitlement to income-related ESA.

Someone is also considered to be on income-related ESA on the following.

pp239-40   HB Regs reg 6 – Remunerative work
Para (7) amended by art 17(3) of the Shared Parental Leave and Statutory Shared Parental Pay (Consequential Amendments to Subordinate Legislation) Order 2014 SI No.3255 as from 31 December 2014. Note: transitional provision is made under art 35.

pp279-325   HB Regs reg 10 – Persons from abroad

[p282: After "(5) Those in receipt of IS or on an income-related ESA: para (3B)(k), add:]

(6) Those in receipt of income- based JSA who have a right to reside other than that as a jobseeker: para 3B(l).

[p296: After first complete paragraph ending in "undue" add:]

In an interim decision in *FT v (1) Islington LB and (2) SSWP (HB)* [2015] UKUT 121 (AAC) given on 6 March 2015, the Upper Tribunal found that a gap of six weeks between the claimant ceasing employment and claiming JSA was not sufficient to break the retention of worker status. The judge observes the case may be useful from "a practitioner's point of view", as an aide to understanding how the principle in *SSWP v MK (IS)* should be applied. The SSWP (and local authority) conceded in that case that they would not argue that a gap of six weeks was down to undue delay. The reasons given by the SSWP were:
> "(a)   the appellant's history of looking for, and speedily obtaining, jobs previously;
> (b)   the availability of existing savings to tide her over; and
> (c)   the evidence provided by the backdating claim form, containing very specific details of the steps which this appellant had taken at the time to look for work and confirmation of the SSWP's view at the time that what she had said was reliable."

The judge (para 15) stated that a key bit of evidence in the case before him (about a HB matter) had to be obtained from the DWP – he does this to draw attention to local authority submission writers, claimant representatives and tribunals that this may be source of evidence in similar cases.

[p297: Immediately before last paragraph before heading [1.5], add:]

SSWP v LL (SPC) [2014] UKUT 136 (AAC) makes the point that the family member of someone is themselves a mere jobseeker – ie, who does not retain worker status through jobseeking, does not have a right of residence sufficient to avoid being a person from abroad.

[p298: After first paragraph, add:]

The correctness of the decision in *ID v SSWP (IS)* doubted in the above paragraph, was considered by the Upper Tribunal in *TG v SSWP (PC)* [2015] UKUT 50 (AAC) under "ISSUE A" of that decision, characterised by the judge as follows.
> "Does the requirement in Article 17(1)(a) of the Directive for a person to "have resided [in another Member State] continuously for more than three years" at the material time refer to actual residence or to residence that is in accordance with specific legal instruments (the point equally apples to the IEEA Regulations)?"

The Upper Tribunal reviewed the history of Article 17 in previous instruments (eg, Regulation (EEC) 1251/70 referred to above). The tribunal also considered *MAH (dual nationality – permanent residence) (Canada)* [2010] UKUT 445 (IAC), para 26 of which stated that there was no requirement that residence be in accordance with the regulations in order to come within the definition of reg

5(1) of the I(EEA) Regs 2006. *MAH* was a three-judge panel of the Upper Tribunal's Immigration and Asylum Chamber. The tribunal notes that *MAH* was not cited to the judge in *ID v SSWP*. The Upper Tribunal holds that it should follow *MAH* (either as it is bound to follow the decision of a three-judge panel from another Chamber or as a matter of comity and in recognition of the seniority of the judges who dealt with that case (which included the Chamber President)). For that, and other reasons which are expounded in detail, the Upper Tribunal in *TG v SSWP (PC)* finds that the residence needed to come within reg 5(1) or Article 17 does not have to be residence that is in accordance with the I(EEA) Regs or the Directive. *ID v SSWP (IS)* should, therefore, no longer be followed.

[p303: At the end of the indented paragraph immediately before heading [1.7], add:]

(The Upper Tribunal has now done so in *TG v SSWP (PC)* [2015] UKUT 50 (AAC). It has decided that the extension of the A8 scheme for the period after 30 April 2009 was unlawful and, hence, that any work done after that date must be regarded as legal work regardless of whether it was registered.)

[p304: Immediately before heading [2], add:]

[1.10] Paragraph (3B)(I): Claimants in receipt of income-based JSA with a non-excluded right of residence

This paragraph applies to those who are in receipt of income-based JSA and who have a right of residence other than as a jobseeker (practically it would be a right "in addition to"). The effect is that such persons can therefore not be excluded from entitlement to HB on the basis that they are not "habitually resident in fact" (see [3] below at p320).

[p313: Immediately before paragraph commenicing "In NA (Pakistan)", add a new paragraph:]

In Case C-218/14 *Kuldip Singh, Denzel Njume, Khaled Aly v Minister for Justice and Equality*, the ECJ has been asked, by an Irish Court, to consider the following questions (the other questions referred relates to a different issue):
> (1) Where marriage involving EU and non-EU citizens ends in divorce obtained following departure of the EU citizen from a host Member State where EU rights were exercised by the EU citizen, and where Articles 7 and 13(2)(a) of Council Directive 2004/38/EC apply, does the non-EU citizen retain a right of residence in the host Member State thereafter? If the answer is in the negative: does the non-EU citizen have a right of residence in the host Member State during the period before divorce following departure of the EU citizen from the host Member State?

The Advocate General's opinion was given on 7 May 2015 and proposes the following answer to this question.
> "Under Directive 2004/38 of the European Parliament and of the Council of 29 April 2004 on the right of citizens of the Union and their family members to move and reside freely within the territory of the Member States, a third-country national loses his right of residence in the host Member State if the Union citizen married to him departs from that Member State, of which she is not a national, even if, at the time of her departure, the marriage had lasted at least three years – including one year in the host State – and was dissolved by decree absolute after the wife's departure to another Member State. Directive 2004/38 does not grant the third-country national any right of residence in the host Member State after the Union citizen's departure, even till the termination of the divorce proceedings by decree absolute."

[p307: In paragraph beginning "The approach to addressing the question...", delete the final sentence of that paragraph.]

[p316: At end of second to last paragraph on page, add:]

This also seems to be the approach suggested by the Advocate General in the recent opinion given in Case C-67/14 *Alimanovic* in which it is again suggested that an individual examination of the facts of the individual's circumstances is what is required.

pp342-47   HB Regs reg B13 – Determination of a maximum rent (social sector)

[p345: In the Analysis of paragraphs (5) and (8), before the paragraph starting "Para (8) includes ...", add:]

MR v North Tyneside Council and SSWP [2015] UKUT 34 (AAC) was a lead case that considered an approach some First-tier Tribunals had adopted to assist claimants faced with a reduction in HB under reg B13. The claimant's son was the subject of a shared residence order and spent time in both parent's houses. The claimant was not receiving child benefit for him, but his other parent was. The local authority decided that as the claimant's son could not be treated as occupying her dwelling, he therefore could not be allowed a bedroom under the size criteria and it reduced her HB accordingly. The First-tier Tribunal, treating the words "dwelling" and "home" in reg B13(5) as undefined ordinary words, decided that the claimant's son occupied her dwelling on a continuing basis with temporary weekly absences and that he occupied his other parent's home on the same basis – ie, the son had more than one home, lived in more than one household and occupied more than one property on a normal basis. Judge Jacobs allowed the local authority's appeal. The meanings of the words used in para (5) are not freestanding but have to be read in the context of other HB provisions, in particular reg 7(1)(a) that treats a claimant who is a member of a "family" as occupying as her/his home, the dwelling s/he normally occupies as a home with her/his "family" (defined in s137(1) SSCBA 1992) and reg 20(2), which deals with situations where a child spends equal amounts of time in different households.

[p345: In the Analysis, under the heading "Bedroom", after the second paragraph, add:]

In *SSWP v Nelson and Nelson* [2014] UKUT 525 (AAC), the First-tier Tribunal had decided that a room that had been classified as a bedroom was not a bedroom because the floor area was too small. A three-judge panel considered the approach that should be taken in determining what a bedroom is for the purposes of reg B13 (what the judges referred to as the "bedroom criteria").

The Upper Tribunal said that when an ordinary or familiar word is used in a statutory test and is not defined, the well established approach is that the test should not be re-written or paraphrased, and the word should be construed and applied in its context having regard to the underlying purposes of the legislation. Applying this approach to reg B13, it decided that in considering whether an HB claimant is under-occupying her/his home:

(1)   the use or potential use of a room can be by any of the people listed in paras (5) and (6);

(2)   consideration must be given to whether the room could be used by any of the people listed in paras (5) or (6). This is because the test is focused on the availability of rooms that could be used as bedrooms by any of those people. However, the Upper Tribunal did not agree that a bedroom must generally be reasonably fit for full-time occupation as a bedroom, as opposed to short-term or irregular occupation by a visitor or overnight guest; *and*

(3)   the occupiers' designation or choices as to which person (or people) should occupy which rooms as bedrooms or how rooms should be used is unlikely to have an impact on the application of reg B13.

Although the starting point in deciding how many bedrooms a home contains is the description of the property by the person renting it out, the Upper Tribunal said (at paragraph 31) that "when an issue arises as to whether a particular room falls to be treated as a bedroom that could be used by any of the persons listed in Regulation B13 (5) and (6) a number of case sensitive factors will need to be considered including (a) size, configuration and overall dimensions, (b) access, (c) natural and electric lighting, (d) ventilation, and (e) privacy."

Note that in the First-tier Tribunal's reasons for its decision, it had suggested that under occupancy was the flip side of overcrowding and that if Parliament had intended that the long-standing statutory minimum standards on overcrowding should be disregarded by the tribunal, it would have been clearly stated in the HB legislation. The Upper Tribunal did not agree.

[p347: In the Analysis of paragraphs (6) and (7), before the final paragraph starting "In the meantime…", add:]

An attempt by a claimant housed under a Sanctuary Scheme to challenge the "social sector" rules was unsuccessful: *R (A) v SSWP* [2015] EWHC 159 (Admin), 29 January 2015. The claimant's HB had been reduced because she was deemed to be underoccupying her home under reg B13. The problem for the claimant was not that she required an additional bedroom, but that she would have to move from her home, specially adapted for her under a Sanctuary Scheme, because she could not afford the HB shortfall. Sanctuary Schemes provide for properties to be adapted (eg, by provision of a secured room) to provide security for people threatened with violence. Under the schemes, a quick police response is ensured, and specialist support is provided.

The claimant made an application for judicial review of the SSWP's failure to provide an appropriate exception for HB recipients who are victims of domestic violence living in accommodation adapted under the provisions of a Sanctuary Scheme. The application was made on the grounds that (1) the HB Regs discriminate against women contrary to Article 14 of the ECHR taken together with Articles 3 and/or 8 and/or Article 1 Protocol 1, (2) the SSWP had failed to comply with his public sector equality duty under s149 of the Equality Act 2010 and (3) the system (that is the combination of the HB Regs and DHPs) is unlawful because it carries, inherent within it, an unacceptable risk of breaches of Article 8 ECHR.

The Court accepted that the rules were discriminatory, but, following *R (MA)* and later decisions, decided that the discrimination was justified – ie, that the SSWP had established that it is not irrational or manifestly without reasonable foundation to have adopted a locally administered scheme of discretionary payments (DHPs) to deal with the issues for HB which arise for those helped under Sanctuary Schemes. The court also decided that the SSWP did enough to satisfy his public sector equality duty.

pp373-74 **HB Regs reg 20 – Circumstances in which a person is to be treated as responsible or not responsible for another**

[p374: In the Analysis of paragraph (2), at the end of the first paragraph numbered (2), add:]

In granting permission to appeal in *Walsall Metropolitan Borough Council v UM (HB)* [2015] UKUT 99 (AAC), Judge Jacobs raised the issue of when a question arose. He said: "This is a difficult expression to understand. Paragraph (2) has to be interpreted in the context of the regulation as a whole. It must not be interpreted in a way that renders other paragraphs redundant. It is not an excuse for a local authority to avoid the need to investigate. It clearly applies if, having investigated, there is no evidence on the matter or if the evidence is insufficient for the local authority or tribunal to make a soundly based finding."

pp387-91 **HB Regs reg 28 – Treatment of child care charges**
Para (14) amended by art 17(4)(a), (b), (c)(iii), (d)(ii) and (e)(ii) of the Shared Parental Leave and Statutory Shared Parental Pay (Consequential Amendments to Subordinate Legislation) Order 2014 SI No.3255 as from 31 December 2014. Para (14) amended by art 17(4)(c)(1) and (ii), (d)(i) and (e)(i) of that order as from 5 April 2015. Note: transitional provision is made under art 35.

pp394-95 **HB Regs reg 29 – Average weekly earnings of employed earners**
Para (12) amended by reg 2(2) of the Housing Benefit and Housing Benefit (Persons who have attained the qualifying age for state pension credit) (Income from earnings) (Amendment) Regulations 2015 SI No.6 as from 9 February 2015.

p396 **HB Regs new reg 29A – Date on which income consisting of earnings from employment as an employed earner are taken into account**
New reg 29A inserted by reg 2(3) of the Housing Benefit and Housing Benefit (Persons who have attained the qualifying age for state pension credit) (Income from earnings) (Amendment) Regulations 2015 SI No.6 as from 9 February 2015.

p399 **HB Regs reg 34 – Disregard of changes in tax, contributions etc**
Para (c) amended by reg 33(2) of the Social Security (Miscellaneous Amendments No.2) Regulations 2015 SI No.478 as from 6 April 2015.

p400   **HB Regs reg 35 – Earnings of employed earners**
Para (1) amended by art 17(5)(ii) and (b) of the Shared Parental Leave and Statutory Shared Parental Pay (Consequential Amendments to Subordinate Legislation) Order 2014 SI No.3255 as from 31 December 2014. Para (1) amended by reg 17(5)(a)(i) of those regulations as from 5 April 2015. Note: transitional provision is made under art 35.

p404   **HB Regs reg 36 – Calculation of net earnings of employed earners**
Para (3) amended by art 17(6)(b) of the Shared Parental Leave and Statutory Shared Parental Pay (Consequential Amendments to Subordinate Legislation) Order 2014 SI No.3255 as from 31 December 2014. Para (3) amended by reg 17(6)(a) of those regulations as from 5 April 2015. Note: transitional provision is made under art 35.

p410   **HB Regs reg 39 – Deduction of tax and contributions of self-employed earners**
Para (2) amended by reg 33(3) of the Social Security (Miscellaneous Amendments No.2) Regulations 2015 SI No.478 as from 6 April 2015.

pp414-17   **HB Regs reg 42 – Notional income**
Para (7)(ce) inserted by reg 15 of Jobseeker's Allowance (18–21 Work Skills Pilot Scheme) Regulations 2014 SI No.3117 as from 25 November 2014, in pilot areas only.

pp426-31   **HB Regs reg 49 – Notional capital**
Para (4)(be) inserted by reg 16 of the Jobseeker's Allowance (18–21 Work Skills Pilot Scheme) Regulations 2014 SI No.3117 as from 25 November 2014, in pilot areas only.

[p430: In the Analysis of paragraph (1), the first issue, "purpose", after the paragraph numbered (4), add a new paragraph:]

In *VW v SSWP (IS)* [2015] UKUT 51 (AAC), Judge Rowland pointed out that in determining whether repayment of a debt to a friend or relative amounts to a deprivation of capital for the purpose of securing or increasing entitlement to benefit, decision makers and tribunals may need to investigate the facts thoroughly and obtain relevant evidence. He said, for example, that evidence may be required on whether there was a loan giving rise to a legally-enforceable debt, as well as evidence of the transfer to the claimant of the money that was lent and of the transfer of money to the alleged lender. A claimant's word can be accepted without corroboration. However, the judge said that "it may be reasonable to expect a friend or relative to provide written and documentary evidence in support of a claimant who claims they were both parties to a legitimate transaction involving a substantial amount of money."

pp436-37   **HB Regs reg 52 – Calculation of tariff income from capital**
Para (8)(a) amended by art 2 and Sch para 24(2) of the Care Act 2014 (Consequential Amendments) (Secondary Legislation) Order 2015 SI No.643 as from 1 April 2015.

pp438-41   **HB Regs reg 53 – Interpretation**
Definitions of "access funds" and "full-time course of study" amended by art 2 and Sch 3 para 8(3) of the Deregulation Act 2015 (Consequential Amendments) Order 2015 SI No.971 as from 26 May 2015.

pp453-54   **HB Regs reg 59 – Calculation of grant income**
Para (4) amended by reg 6 of the Social Security (Miscellaneous Amendments) Regulations 2015 SI No.67 as from 23 February 2015.

pp477-78   **HB Regs Part 8A General Note – Benefit cap**

[p478: At the end of the penultimate paragraph of the commentary on challenging a benefit cap starting "A challenge…", add:]

The claimants had all experienced extreme domestic violence and abuse and were in danger of becoming homeless as a result of the benefit cap.

[p478: For the final paragraph of the commentary on challenging a benefit cap, substitute:]

The claimants appealed to the Supreme Court: *R (SG and others (previously JS and others)) v SSWP* [2015] UKSC 16, 18 March 2015. Although the Supreme Court found that in introducing the benefit cap the government had failed to comply with the UN Convention on the Rights of the Child, in a 3:2 split decision, it decided that the benefit cap did not breach Article 14 of the Convention and that it is, therefore, lawful.

pp480-81   HB Regs reg 75E – Exception to the benefit cap: current or recent work
Para (4) amended by art 17(7) of the Shared Parental Leave and Statutory Shared Parental Pay (Consequential Amendments to Subordinate Legislation) Order 2014 SI No.3255 as from 31 December 2014. Note: transitional provision is made under art 35.

pp612-29   HB Regs Sch 5 – Sums to be disregarded in the calculation of income other than earnings
Para A5 inserted by reg 17 of Jobseeker's Allowance (18–21 Work Skills Pilot Scheme) Regulations 2014 SI No.3117 as from 25 November 2014, in pilot areas only.

Para 27(dza) inserted and para 57 amended by art 2 and Sch para 24(3) of the Care Act 2014 (Consequential Amendments) (Secondary Legislation) Order 2015 SI No.643 as from 1 April 2015.

pp629-45   HB Regs Sch 6 – Capital to be disregarded
Para A5 inserted by reg 18 of Jobseeker's Allowance (18–21 Work Skills Pilot Scheme) Regulations 2014 SI No.3117 as from 25 November 2014, in pilot areas only.

Para 58 amended by art 2 and Sch para 24(4) of the Care Act 2014 (Consequential Amendments) (Secondary Legislation) Order 2015 SI No.643 as from 1 April 2015.

pp662-73   HB (SPC) Regs reg 2 – Interpretation
In Scotland, definition of "couple" substituted by Sch 6 para 28 of the Marriage and Civil Partnership (Scotland) Act 2014 and Civil Partnership Act 2004 (Consequential Provisions and Modifications) Order 2014 SI No.3229 as from 16 December 2014.

Definition of "shared parental leave" inserted by art 18(2)(b) of the Shared Parental Leave and Statutory Shared Parental Pay (Consequential Amendments to Subordinate Legislation) Order 2014 SI No.3255 as from 31 December 2014. Definition of "paternity leave" amended by art 18(2)(a) of those regulations as from 5 April 2015. Note: transitional provision is made under art 35.

Para (6)(ab) inserted and para (6)(b) amended by reg 2(2) of the Social Security (Miscellaneous Amendments) Regulations 2015 SI No.67 as from 23 February 2015.

Definition of "training allowance" amended by art 2 and Sch 3 para 9 of the Deregulation Act 2015 (Consequential Amendments) Order 2015 SI No.971 as from 26 May 2015.

p676   HB(SPC) Regs reg 6 – Remunerative work
Para (7) amended by art 18(3) of the Shared Parental Leave and Statutory Shared Parental Pay (Consequential Amendments to Subordinate Legislation) Order 2014 SI No.3255 as from 31 December 2014. Note: transitional provision is made under art 35.

pp707-09   HB(SPC) Regs reg 29 – Meaning of "income"
Para (1) amended by art 18(4)(c) of the Shared Parental Leave and Statutory Shared Parental Pay (Consequential Amendments to Subordinate Legislation) Order 2014 SI No.3255 as from 31 December 2014. Para (1) amended by art 18(4)(a) and (b) of that order as from 5 April 2015. Note: transitional provision is made under art 35.

pp711-14   HB(SPC) Regs reg 31 – Treatment of child care charges
Paras (14) and (15) amended by art 18(5)(a), (b), (c)(iii), (d)(ii) and (e)(ii) of the Shared Parental Leave and Statutory Shared Parental Pay (Consequential Amendments to Subordinate Legislation) Order 2014 SI No.3255 as from 31 December 2014. Paras (14) and (15) amended by art 18(5)

(c)(i) and (ii), (d)(i) and (e)(i) of that order as from 5 April 2015. Note: transitional provision is made under art 35.

pp715-16   HB (SPC) Regs reg 33 – Calculation of weekly income
Para (1) amended and paras (2A) and (3A) inserted by reg 3 of the Housing Benefit and Housing Benefit (Persons who have attained the qualifying age for state pension credit) (Income from earnings) (Amendment) Regulations 2015 SI No.6 as from 9 February 2015.

p717   HB (SPC) Regs reg 34 – Disregard of changes in tax, contributions etc
Para (c) amended by reg 34(2) of the Social Security (Miscellaneous Amendments No.2) Regulations 2015 SI No.478 as from 6 April 2015.

pp717-18   HB(SPC) Regs reg 35 – Earnings of employed earners
Para (1) amended by art 18(6)(c) of the Shared Parental Leave and Statutory Shared Parental Pay (Consequential Amendments to Subordinate Legislation) Order 2014 SI No.3255 as from 31 December 2014. Para (1) amended by art 18(6)(a) and (b) of that order as from 5 April 2015. Note: transitional provision is made under art 35.

pp718-19   HB(SPC) Regs reg 36 – Calculation of net earnings of employed earners
Para (2) amended by art 18(7)(b) of the Shared Parental Leave and Statutory Shared Parental Pay (Consequential Amendments to Subordinate Legislation) Order 2014 SI No.3255 as from 31 December 2014. Para (2) amended by art 18(7)(a) of that order as from 5 April 2015. Note: transitional provision is made under art 35.

p720   HB(SPC) Regs reg 38 – Earnings of self-employed earners
Para (2)(d) amended by art 2 and Sch para 25(2) of the Care Act 2014 (Consequential Amendments) (Secondary Legislation) Order 2015 SI No.643 as from 1 April 2015.

p717   HB (SPC) Regs reg 40 – Deduction of tax and contributions of self-employed earners
Para (2) amended by reg 34(3) of the Social Security (Miscellaneous Amendments No.2) Regulations 2015 SI No.478 as from 6 April 2015.

pp795-802   HB(SPC) Regs Sch 6 – Capital to be disregarded
Para 26D amended by art 2 and Sch para 25(3) of the Care Act 2014 (Consequential Amendments) (Secondary Legislation) Order 2015 SI No.643 as from 1 April 2015.

pp817-18   RO(HBF) Order art 4B – Broad rental market area determinations and local housing allowance determinations
Para (2B) substituted by art 2(2) of the Rent Officers (Housing Benefit and Universal Credit Functions) (Local Housing Allowance Amendments) Order 2014 SI No.3126 as from 8 January 2015.

pp831-36   RO(HBF) Order Sch 3B – Broad rental market area determinations and local housing allowance determinations
Tables in paras 2(9) and 6 substituted by art 2(3) and Sch 1 of the Rent Officers (Housing Benefit and Universal Credit Functions) (Local Housing Allowance Amendments) Order 2014 SI No.3126 as from 8 January 2015.

pp841-42   RO(HBF) (Scotland) Order Art 4B – Broad rental market area determinations and local housing allowance determinations
Para (2B) substituted by art 3(2) of the Rent Officers (Housing Benefit and Universal Credit Functions) (Local Housing Allowance Amendments) Order 2014 SI No.3126 as from 8 January 2015.

pp853-56 RO(HBF) (Scotland) Order Sch 3B – Broad rental market area determinations and local housing allowance determinations

Tables in paras 2(9) and 6 substituted by art 3(3) and Sch 2 of the Rent Officers (Housing Benefit and Universal Credit Functions) (Local Housing Allowance Amendments) Order 2014 SI No.3126 as from 8 January 2015.

pp859-61 D&A Regs reg 1 – Citation, commencement and Interpretation

In Scotland, definition of "couple" substituted by Sch 6 para 21 of the Marriage and Civil Partnership (Scotland) Act 2014 and Civil Partnership Act 2004 (Consequential Provisions and Modifications) Order 2014 SI No.3229 as from 16 December 2014.

pp917-19 TP(FTT) Rules r5 – Case management powers

[p919: In the General Note, before the final paragraph, add:]

If the First-tier Tribunal decides an issue in the proceedings as a preliminary issue under r5(3)(e), its decision on that issue is binding (subject to any appeal or application under Part 4 of the TP(FTT) Rules) on the parties and on any tribunal that subsequently decides other issues in the same proceedings even if that tribunal is differently constituted from the tribunal that decided the preliminary issue. It is to be contrasted with an interim decision in which the First-tier Tribunal or Upper Tribunal makes a decision on some of the issues – or in respect of part of the period – before it, but adjourns the other issues – or periods – to be decided by the same tribunal on a later date.

There is some dispute whether it is possible for the First-tier Tribunal to decide an issue as a preliminary issue without there first having been a formal direction that the issue should be dealt with in that way. The answer depends upon whether r5(3) is read as giving examples of the type of directions that may be given under r5(2) or whether it is read as giving examples of the ways in which the First-tier Tribunal may regulate its own procedure under r5(1), some – but not necessarily all – of which will require directions to be given under r5(2). The latter is the better view, particularly as r5(3) is expressed as not restricting the general powers conferred by both rr5(1) and (2). However, the dispute is academic because even if – contrary to the view expressed in the previous sentence – a direction is necessary, r5(2) provides that the necessary direction can be given "at any time". So a tribunal that decided in the course of a hearing that it was appropriate to deal with an issue as a preliminary issue could give the necessary direction there and then, subject to its being in accordance with the overriding objective to do so.

The more important question is whether it is ever appropriate for the First-tier Tribunal to proceed in that way. In *R (SB and others) v First-tier Tribunal and CICA* [2014] UKUT 497 (AAC) (a judicial review of a number of decisions of the First-tier Tribunal relating to criminal injuries compensation) a three-judge panel of the Upper Tribunal suggests that it might be. The panel states:

"104. We recognise, however, that if the terms of a CICA review decision were to encompass determinations in respect of eligibility and the level of compensation then on an appeal against such a decision a FtT may be required to decide both issues… In such an example we can see that in some circumstances it may be sensible for the FtT to hold separate hearings on the two issues under appeal. We are cautious about seeking to give detailed guidance as to how the FtT should approach such a scenario given it is hypothetical and none of the parties made detailed or contested arguments on this issue. We therefore confine ourselves to drawing attention to the provisions of rule 5(3)(e) of the FtT's procedure rules – "the Tribunal may deal with an issue in the proceedings as a preliminary issue" – and observe that if this rule is invoked and the preliminary issue decided then the time limit for judicial review of that decision would run from the date of the decision or written reasons being given for it: per r.28(2) and (3)(a) of the Tribunal Procedure (Upper Tribunal) Rules 2008.

105. Care may therefore need to be taken by the FtT when faced with deciding more than one issue on an appeal. In the case of Ms Barrett it was (and is) possible that determining the tariff and loss of earnings levels of compensation could be addressed separately at different hearings. If the appeal hearing genuinely goes part heard (e.g. the FtT intended to address both issues but simply runs

out of time), and it is therefore adjourned to be heard by the same FtT members (and doing so would not unnecessarily delay the final resolution of the appeal), then it would seem to us that, whatever preliminary view the FtT may have come to on the first issue (e.g. the level of the tariff award), no decision would be made until the further hearing has taken place. The time limit for applying for judicial review would therefore not begin to run until the decision made at the second (or final) hearing.

106. On the other hand, it may be clear at the outset of the first hearing, or even during the course of that hearing, that only one issue can sensibly be determined, and the FtT may then wish to use the r.5(3)(e) power to finally decide that issue (e.g. where it may not be possible to reconvene the same tribunal membership within an appropriate time)."

However, there is a tension between that approach and what has been said about the use of preliminary issues by judges of the House of Lords in *Tilling v Whiteman* [1980] AC 1 at 17F-18A and 25B-C, of the Court of Appeal in *McLoughlin and Jones* [2002] QB 1312 at para 66, and of the High Court in *Steele v Steele* [2001] CP Rep 106. In particular, in *McLoughlin v Jones*, David Steel J stated:

"66. In my judgment, the right approach to preliminary issues should be as follows. (a) Only issues which are decisive or potentially decisive should be identified. (b) The questions should usually be questions of law. (c) They should be decided on the basis of a schedule of agreed or assumed facts. (d) They should be triable without significant delay, making full allowance for the implications of a possible appeal. (e) Any order should be made by the court following a case management conference."

As noted by Upper Tribunal Judge Jacobs, writing extra-judicially in *Tribunal Practice and Procedure: Tribunals under the Tribunals* (Third Edition, Legal Action Group, London 2014) at p317 para 7.172 (Courts and Enforcement Act 2007), the final requirement may be less appropriate in the tribunal context. However, the approach set out in the first four requirements is very different to the approach of the Upper Tribunal in *R (SB and others)* under which, it is contemplated that it may be appropriate to decide a preliminary issue merely to avoid going part-heard.

pp920-25   TP(FTT) Rules r8 – Striking out a party's case

[p924: In the Analysis of r8(3)(c), under the heading "No reasonable prospects of success: paras (3)(c) and (4)", immediately before the final paragraph, add:]

An application to strike out an appeal as having no prospects of success should normally be accompanied by a full response, complying with r24(4), and that response must be copied to the claimant by the decision maker: see *JT v HMRC (TC)* [2015] UKUT 81 (AAC) at para 22 where Judge Rowland stated:

"22. An application for the striking out of an appeal can be distinguished from a response to an appeal but, except where providing a full response would clearly be disproportionate, there are several reasons why an application for the striking out of an appeal under rule 8(3)(c) on the ground that it has no prospects of success should be accompanied by a full response and should be copied to the claimant. First, it is obviously difficult for the First-tier Tribunal to decide whether an appeal has any prospects of success unless it has a substantial amount of information about the merits of the appeal. Secondly, rule 8(4) requires the First-tier Tribunal to give the appellant an opportunity to make representations in relation to the proposed striking out and the claimant needs a copy of the application in order to make effective representations. Striking an appeal out rather than determining it is not likely to be justified unless there will be a saving of time and money and requiring the First-tier Tribunal to send the claimant the application rather than the decision maker doing it is likely to be both time-consuming and more costly. Thirdly, and again in the interests of saving time and money, the provision of a response with an application for striking out enables the First-tier Tribunal to proceed to list the case for determination straightaway if not minded to strike it out."

pp932-33 **TP(FTT) Rules r23 – Cases in which the notice of appeal is to be sent to the decision maker**

[p933: In the General Note on r23(6), delete the final paragraph on the page, and after "(2) The notice must be signed by the appellant," add:]

This requirement is also met if the notice is signed by the appellant's solicitor: see *CO v LB Havering (CH)* [2015] UKUT 28 (AAC) at paras 22–31. In *R v Lambeth LBC ex p Crookes* [1998] 31 HLR 59, QBD, the High Court had held that an equivalent requirement in reg 79(2) of the Housing Benefit (General) Regulations 1987 could only be satisfied by the personal signature of the claimant. However, as noted in previous editions, the decision in *Crookes* strongly relied upon the decision of the Court of Appeal in *re Prince Blucher* [1931] 2 Ch D 70, which was held to have been wrongly decided by the Privy Council in *General Legal Council ex p Basil Whitter v Barrington Earl Frankson* [2006] UKPC 42. In those circumstances, Upper Tribunal Judge Wikeley declined in *CO* to follow *Crookes* and that decision is now binding on the First-tier Tribunal.

Where the notice is signed by a representative who does not hold a professional qualification, such as a CAB adviser or a local authority welfare rights worker, the position is more complex. If the representative provides a letter of authority signed by the claimant then, "for the purposes of rule 26(3) they are, in practical terms, in the same position as a solicitor who writes on the instructions of their client": see *CO* at para 30. If no authority is provided, it cannot always be assumed that the representative is acting on the claimant's instructions. However, it is suggested that where subsequent investigation establishes that the representative did have authority, it will usually be appropriate for the tribunal to waive the failure to comply with the requirement for the claimant's signature under r7 TP(FTT) Rules.

pp934-37 **TP(FTT) Rules r24 – Responses and replies**

[p935: In the General Note on r24(4)(b), in the second paragraph under the heading "Head (b)", after "... they do not assist the authority's case", add:]

The obligation to provide copies of relevant documents is not "cut down by consideration of what the appellant might have in his or her possession and be able to put before the tribunal": see *ST v SSWP (ESA)* [2012] UKUT 469 (AAC) at para 25.

[p935: In the General Note on r24(4)(b), after the insertion above add a paragraph break (ie, so that the words "It will be particularly important..." begin a new paragraph. Then, at the end of that paragraph, add:]

In overpayment cases where there has been an interview under caution, the transcript of that interview is a relevant document and must be produced to the tribunal by the local authority: see *LM v LB Southwark (HB)* [2015] UKUT 86 (AAC) at paras 35–43.

pp937-39 **TP(FTT) Rules r27 – Decision with or without a hearing**

[p937: In the General Note, after the paragraph starting "the duty to hold a hearing ....", add:]

In cases where a claimant has asked for a decision on the papers because s/he is unable to attend a hearing in person (eg, for reasons of ill-health such as agoraphobia), the overriding objective may require the tribunal to attempt to overcome that inability "by considering whether her participation in the hearing could have been facilitated, for instance by offering to her/him the opportunity to participate by telephone or skype, or explaining to her/him that taxi fares could be reimbursed": see *LC v SSWP (DLA)* [2015] UKUT 100 (AAC) at para 10.

pp939-40 **TP(FTT) Rules r30 – Public and private hearings**

[p940: At the end of the General Note, add:]

The minimum requirement of a public hearing, is that it takes place within reasonable office hours and at a publicly recognised court or tribunal hearing centre. It is not necessary for the hearing to be publicised in advance, or for a list of scheduled public hearings to be on display at that centre, except where the absence of publicity can be shown to be a stratagem to deprive a claimant of a public hearing in a particular case: see *DF v SSWP (ESA)* [2015] UKUT 143 (AAC).

pp941-42   TP(FTT) Rules r34 – Reasons for decisions

[p942: In the General Note, after the penultimate paragraph, add:]

A decision to refuse an extension of the time limit in r34(4) – and, by implication, also a decision to grant one – is a decision within s11 TCEA and can therefore be appealed to the Upper Tribunal and set aside under s9, if it is made in error of law. The TP(FTT) Rules do not require a judge who refuses – or grants – an extension of time to provide reasons for that decision. However, any reasons in fact given can be taken into account when deciding whether there has been an error of law: see *HP v SSWP (ESA)* [2014] UKUT 491 (AAC) and *RU v SSWP (ESA)* [2014] UKUT 532 (AAC).

pp945-46   TP(FTT) Rules r38 – Application for permission to appeal

[p946: Turn the final sentence in the General Note into a new paragraph and add the following at the end of the previous paragraph:]

Rule 38(7)(c) requires the tribunal to consider whether or not to admit the application for permission to appeal in all cases in which there is no written statement of reasons because of delay in applying for one: see *HP v SSWP (ESA)* [2014] UKUT 491 (AAC) at paras 23–25.

p949   TP(FTT) Rules r41 – Power to treat an application as a different type of application

[p949: Add a new General Note:]

General Note

It will often be unclear what application an unrepresented appellant intends to make. In such circumstances, the tribunal, in the exercise of its enabling jurisdiction, should interpret what has been written as being whatever application gives the claimant the best chance of achieving what s/he wants under the TP(FTT) Rules. It may sometimes be necessary to seek clarification from the claimant about what s/he is asking for.

Rule 41 serves a different purpose. Even where a party has unequivocally applied for a particular remedy under Part 4 of the Rules, the tribunal may treat that application as being for a different remedy. So, for example, if a party has applied for permission to appeal to the Upper Tribunal, but the judge considering that application decides that the conditions in r37 for the First-tier Tribunal's decision to be set aside on procedural grounds are satisfied, s/he may instead treat the application as being for the decision to be set aside. As with all discretionary powers under the rules, this power must be exercised having regard to the overriding objective of dealing with cases fairly and justly. It is, therefore, necessary for the judge to consider whether or not to treat the application as being a different application in every case in which a post-hearing application is made and there will be occasions on which the overriding objective will require the judge to take that course: see *DC v SSWP (ESA)* [2015] UKUT 150 (AAC) at paras 26–33.

pp1005-07   Local Government Finance Act 1992 Schedule 1A para 3 – Preparation of a scheme

[p1006: At the end of the penultimate paragraph add the following:]

For a discussion of *Mosely*, see *R (on the application of T) v Trafford Metropolitan Borough Council* [2015] EWHC 369 (Admin).

pp1015-21   The Council Tax Reduction Schemes (Prescribed Requirements) (England) Regulations 2012 reg 2 – Interpretation
Definition of "contributory employment and support allowance" substituted, definition of "service user group" omitted and para (8) inserted by reg 2(2) of the Council Tax Reduction Schemes

(Prescribed Requirements) (England) (Amendment) (No.2) Regulations 2014 SI No.3312 as from 12 January 2015, in relation to schemes made for financial years starting on or after 1 April 2015.

Definition of "shared parental leave" inserted by art 27(2)(b) of the Shared Parental Leave and Statutory Shared Parental Pay (Consequential Amendments to Subordinate Legislation) Order 2014 SI No.3255 as from 31 December 2014. Definition of "paternity leave" amended inserted by art 27(2)(a) of that order as from 5 April 2015. Note: transitional provision is made under art 35.

Definition of "training allowance" amended by art 2 and Sch 3 para 23 of the Deregulation Act 2015 (Consequential Amendments) Order 2015 SI No.971 as from 26 May 2015.

pp1022-23 **The Council Tax Reduction Schemes (Prescribed Requirements) (England) Regulations 2012 reg 6 – Meaning of "family"**
Para (3)(c) inserted by reg 2(3) of the Council Tax Reduction Schemes (Prescribed Requirements) (England) (Amendment) (No.2) Regulations 2014 SI No.3312 as from 12 January 2015 , in relation to schemes made for financial years starting on or after 1 April 2015.

pp1025-26 **The Council Tax Reduction Schemes (Prescribed Requirements) (England) Regulations 2012 reg 10 – Remunerative work**
Para (7) amended by art 27(3) of the Shared Parental Leave and Statutory Shared Parental Pay (Consequential Amendments to Subordinate Legislation) Order 2014 SI No.3255 as from 31 December 2014. Note: transitional provision is made under art 35.

p1027 **The Council Tax Reduction Schemes (Prescribed Requirements) (England) Regulations 2012 reg 12 – Persons treated as not being in Great Britain**
Para 12(5)(h) amended and para 12(5)(ha) inserted reg 2(4) of the Council Tax Reduction Schemes (Prescribed Requirements) (England) (Amendment) (No.2) Regulations 2014 SI No.3312 as from 12 January 2015 in relation to schemes made for financial years starting on or after 1 April 2015. Note: transitional provision is made in reg 3 of those regulations.

pp1029-59 **The Council Tax Reduction Schemes (Prescribed Requirements) (England) Regulations 2012 Sch 1 – Pensioners: matters that must be included in an authority's scheme**
Amounts in paras 8 uprated and paras 8(8)(c) and (11A) inserted by reg 2(5) of the Council Tax Reduction Schemes (Prescribed Requirements) (England) (Amendment) (No.2) Regulations 2014 SI No.3312 as from 12 January 2015 in relation to schemes made for financial years starting on or after 1 April 2015.

Paras 16, 18, 19 and 25 amended by art 27(4)(a)(iii), (b)(iii), (c), (d)(i) and (iv) and (e) of the Shared Parental Leave and Statutory Shared Parental Pay (Consequential Amendments to Subordinate Legislation) Order 2014 SI No.3255 as from 31 December 2014. Paras 16, 18 and 25 amended by art 27(4)(a)(i) and (ii), (b)(i) and (ii) and (d)(1) and (iv) of that order as from 5 April 2015. Note: transitional provision is made under art 35.

Paras 8(6) and (12), 21(2), 25(13) and 26 amended and para 8(11) inserted by art 2 and Sch para 26(2)–(5) of the Care Act 2014 (Consequential Amendments) (Secondary Legislation) Order 2015 SI No.643 as from 1 April 2015.

pp1059-63 **The Council Tax Reduction Schemes (Prescribed Requirements) (England) Regulations 2012 Sch 2 – Applicable amounts**
Amounts uprated by reg 2(6) of the Council Tax Reduction Schemes (Prescribed Requirements) (England) (Amendment) (No.2) Regulations 2014 SI No.3312 as from 12 January 2015 in relation to schemes made for financial years starting on or after 1 April 2015.

Para 6 amended by art 2 and Sch para 26(6) of the Care Act 2014 (Consequential Amendments) (Secondary Legislation) Order 2015 SI No.643 as from 1 April 2015.

pp1063-64   The Council Tax Reduction Schemes (Prescribed Requirements) (England) Regulations 2012 Sch 3 – Amounts of alternative maximum council tax reduction
Amounts uprated by reg 2(7) of the Council Tax Reduction Schemes (Prescribed Requirements) (England) (Amendment) (No.2) Regulations 2014 SI No.3312 as from 12 January 2015.

pp1064-66   The Council Tax Reduction Schemes (Prescribed Requirements) (England) Regulations 2012 Sch 4 – Sums disregarded from applicant's earnings
Paras 5 and 6 amended by reg 2(8) of the Council Tax Reduction Schemes (Prescribed Requirements) (England) (Amendment) (No.2) Regulations 2014 SI No.3312 as from 12 January 2015 in relation to schemes made for financial years starting on or after 1 April 2015.

Para 5 amended by art 2 and Sch para 26(7) of the Care Act 2014 (Consequential Amendments) (Secondary Legislation) Order 2015 SI No.643 as from 1 April 2015.

pp1067-69   The Council Tax Reduction Schemes (Prescribed Requirements) (England) Regulations 2012 Sch 5 – Amounts to be disregarded in the calculation of income other than earnings
Amounts in para 19 uprated by reg 2(9) of the Council Tax Reduction Schemes (Prescribed Requirements) (England) (Amendment) (No.2) Regulations 2014 SI No.3312 as from 12 January 2015 in relation to schemes made for financial years starting on or after 1 April 2015.

pp1069-74   The Council Tax Reduction Schemes (Prescribed Requirements) (England) Regulations 2012 Sch 6 – Capital disregards
Paras 21 and 22 amended reg 2(10) of the Council Tax Reduction Schemes (Prescribed Requirements) (England) (Amendment) (No.2) Regulations 2014 SI No.3312 as from 12 January 2015 in relation to schemes made for financial years starting on or after 1 April 2015.

Para 29 amended by art 2 and Sch para 26(8) of the Care Act 2014 (Consequential Amendments) (Secondary Legislation) Order 2015 SI No.643 as from 1 April 2015.

pp1085-93   The Council Tax Reduction Schemes and Prescribed Requirements (Wales) Regulations 2013 Reg 2 – Interpretation
Definition of "contributory employment and support allowance" substituted and definition of "shared parental leave" inserted by reg 3 of the Council Tax Reduction Schemes (Prescribed Requirements and Default Scheme) (Wales) (Amendment) Regulations 2015 SI No.44 (W.3) as from 21 January 2015 in relation to schemes made for financial years starting on or after 1 April 2015.

Definition of "training allowance" amended by art 2 and Sch 3 para 30(2) of the Deregulation Act 2015 (Consequential Amendments) Order 2015 SI No.971 as from 26 May 2015.

Definition of "lwfans hyfforddi" ("training allowance") amended by art 2 and Sch 3 para 30(5) of the Deregulation Act 2015 (Consequential Amendments) Order 2015 SI No.971 as from 26 May 2015.

pp1097-98   The Council Tax Reduction Schemes and Prescribed Requirements (Wales) Regulations 2013 Reg 10 – Remunerative work
Para (7) amended by reg 4 of the Council Tax Reduction Schemes (Prescribed Requirements and Default Scheme) (Wales) (Amendment) Regulations 2015 SI No.44 (W.3) as from 21 January 2015 in relation to schemes made for financial years starting on or after 1 April 2015.

p1099   The Council Tax Reduction Schemes (Prescribed Requirements) (Wales) Regulations 2013 Reg 18 – Revisions to and replacement of schemes
Para (4) amended and para (6) inserted by reg 5 of the Council Tax Reduction Schemes (Prescribed Requirements and Default Scheme) (Wales) (Amendment) Regulations 2015 SI No.44 (W.3) as from 21 January 2015 in relation to schemes made for financial years starting on or after 1 April 2015.

pp1103-05   The Council Tax Reduction Schemes and Prescribed Requirements (Wales) Regulations 2013 Reg 28 – Persons treated as not being in Great Britain
Para (5) amended by reg 6 of the Council Tax Reduction Schemes (Prescribed Requirements and Default Scheme) (Wales) (Amendment) Regulations 2015 SI No.44 (W.3) as from 21 January 2015

in relation to schemes made for financial years starting on or after 1 April 2015. Note: the amendments do not apply to a person who, on 13 March 2013, was liable to pay council tax at a reduced rate by virtue of a council tax reduction scheme and was entitled to income-based jobseeker's allowance (JSA) until the earliest of the date the person makes a new application for a council tax reduction or the date s/he ceases to be entitled to income-based JSA.

pp1108-35 **The Council Tax Reduction Schemes and Prescribed Requirements (Wales) Regulations 2013 Sch 1 – Determining eligibility for a reduction: pensioners**
Paras 3, 12, 13 and 19 amended and amounts uprated by reg 7 of the Council Tax Reduction Schemes (Prescribed Requirements and Default Scheme) (Wales) (Amendment) Regulations 2015 SI No.44 (W.3) as from 21 January 2015 in relation to schemes made for financial years starting on or after 1 April 2015.

pp1135-38 **The Council Tax Reduction Schemes and Prescribed Requirements (Wales) Regulations 2013 Sch 2 – Applicable amounts: pensioners**
Amounts uprated by reg 8 of the Council Tax Reduction Schemes (Prescribed Requirements and Default Scheme) (Wales) (Amendment) Regulations 2015 SI No.44 (W.3) as from 21 January 2015 in relation to schemes made for financial years starting on or after 1 April 2015.

pp1139-41 **The Council Tax Reduction Schemes and Prescribed Requirements (Wales) Regulations 2013 Sch 3 – Sums disregarded from applicant's earnings: pensioners**
Paras 5 and 6 amended by reg 9 of the Council Tax Reduction Schemes (Prescribed Requirements and Default Scheme) (Wales) (Amendment) Regulations 2015 SI No.44 (W.3) as from 21 January 2015 in relation to schemes made for financial years starting on or after 1 April 2015.

pp1148-71 **The Council Tax Reduction Schemes and Prescribed Requirements (Wales) Regulations 2013 Sch 6 – Determining eligibility for a reduction**
Paras 5, 14, 15, 17 and 21 amended and amounts uprated by reg 10 of the Council Tax Reduction Schemes (Prescribed Requirements and Default Scheme) (Wales) (Amendment) Regulations 2015 SI No.44 (W.3) as from 21 January 2015 in relation to schemes made for financial years starting on or after 1 April 2015.

pp1171-79 **The Council Tax Reduction Schemes (Prescribed Requirements) (Wales) Regulations 2013 Sch 7 – Applicable amounts: persons who are not pensioners**
Paras 18 and 23 to 27 amended and amounts uprated by reg 11 of the Council Tax Reduction Schemes (Prescribed Requirements and Default Scheme) (Wales) (Amendment) Regulations 2015 SI No.44 (W.3) as from 21 January 2015 in relation to schemes made for financial years starting on or after 1 April 2015.

pp1170-82 **The Council Tax Reduction Schemes and Prescribed Requirements (Wales) Regulations 2013 Sch 8 – Sums to be disregarded in the calculation of earnings: persons who are not pensioners**
Para 12 amended by reg 12 of the Council Tax Reduction Schemes (Prescribed Requirements and Default Scheme) (Wales) (Amendment) Regulations 2015 SI No.44 (W.3) as from 21 January 2015 in relation to schemes made for financial years starting on or after 1 April 2015.

pp1196-03 **The Council Tax Reduction Schemes and Prescribed Requirements (Wales) Regulations 2013 Sch 11 – Students**
Para 3 amended by reg 13 of the Council Tax Reduction Schemes (Prescribed Requirements and Default Scheme) (Wales) (Amendment) Regulations 2015 SI No.44 (W.3) as from 21 January 2015 in relation to schemes made for financial years starting on or after 1 April 2015.

In para 1, definitions of "access funds" and "full-time course of study" amended by art 2 and Sch 3 para 30(3) of the Deregulation Act 2015 (Consequential Amendments) Order 2015 SI No.971 as from 26 May 2015.

In para 1, definitions of "cronfeydd mynediad" ("access funds") and "cwrs astudio amser llawn" ("full-time course of study") amended by art 2 and Sch 3 para 30(6) of the Deregulation Act 2015 (Consequential Amendments) Order 2015 SI No.971 as from 26 May 2015.

pp1217-23   The Council Tax Reduction Schemes (Default Scheme) (Wales) Regulations 2013
Sch para 2 – Interpretation
Definition of "contributory employment and support allowance" substituted, definition of "paternity leave" amended and definition of "shared parental leave" inserted by reg 15 of the Council Tax Reduction Schemes (Prescribed Requirements and Default Scheme) (Wales) (Amendment) Regulations 2015 SI No.44 (W.3) as from 21 January 2015 in relation to schemes made for financial years starting on or after 1 April 2015.

Definition of "training allowance" amended by art 2 and Sch 3 para 31(2) of the Deregulation Act 2015 (Consequential Amendments) Order 2015 SI No.971 as from 26 May 2015.

Definition of "lwfans hyfforddi" ("training allowance") amended by art 2 and Sch 3 para 31(5) of the Deregulation Act 2015 (Consequential Amendments) Order 2015 SI No.971 as from 26 May 2015.

p1226   The Council Tax Reduction Schemes (Default Scheme) (Wales) Regulations 2013
Sch para 10 – Remunerative work
Sub-para (7) amended by reg 16 of the Council Tax Reduction Schemes (Prescribed Requirements and Default Scheme) (Wales) (Amendment) Regulations 2015 SI No.44 (W.3) as from 21 January 2015 in relation to schemes made for financial years starting on or after 1 April 2015.

pp1229-30   The Council Tax Reduction Schemes (Default Scheme) (Wales) Regulations 2013
Sch para 19 – Class of persons excluded from the scheme: persons treated as not being in Great Britain
Sub-para (5) amended by reg 17 of the Council Tax Reduction Schemes (Prescribed Requirements and Default Scheme) (Wales) (Amendment) Regulations 2015 SI No.44 (W.3) as from 21 January 2015 in relation to schemes made for financial years starting on or after 1 April 2015. Note: the amendments do not apply to a person who, on 13 March 2013, was liable to pay council tax at a reduced rate by virtue of a council tax reduction scheme and was entitled to income-based jobseeker's allowance (JSA) until the earliest of the date the person makes a new application for a council tax reduction or the date s/he ceases to be entitled to income-based JSA.

pp1232-33   The Council Tax Reduction Schemes (Default Scheme) (Wales) Regulations 2013
Sch para 28 – Non-dependant deductions: pensioners and persons who are not pensioners
Sub-para (8) amended, sub-para (10) inserted and amounts uprated by reg 18 of the Council Tax Reduction Schemes (Prescribed Requirements and Default Scheme) (Wales) (Amendment) Regulations 2015 SI No.44 (W.3) as from 21 January 2015 in relation to schemes made for financial years starting on or after 1 April 2015.

pp1235-37   The Council Tax Reduction Schemes (Default Scheme) (Wales) Regulations 2013
Sch para 36 – Meaning of "income": pensioners
Sub-para (1) amended by reg 19 of the Council Tax Reduction Schemes (Prescribed Requirements and Default Scheme) (Wales) (Amendment) Regulations 2015 SI No.44 (W.3) as from 21 January 2015 in relation to schemes made for financial years starting on or after 1 April 2015.

p1238   The Council Tax Reduction Schemes (Default Scheme) (Wales) Regulations 2013
Sch para 38 – Earnings of employed earners: pensioners
Sub-para (1)(ja) inserted by reg 20 of the Council Tax Reduction Schemes (Prescribed Requirements and Default Scheme) (Wales) (Amendment) Regulations 2015 SI No.44 (W.3) as from 21 January 2015 in relation to schemes made for financial years starting on or after 1 April 2015.

pp1238-39 The Council Tax Reduction Schemes (Default Scheme) (Wales) Regulations 2013
Sch para 39 – Calculation of net earnings of employed earners: pensioners
Sub-para (2)(d) amended by reg 21 of the Council Tax Reduction Schemes (Prescribed Requirements and Default Scheme) (Wales) (Amendment) Regulations 2015 SI No.44 (W.3) as from 21 January 2015 in relation to schemes made for financial years starting on or after 1 April 2015.

pp1242-43 The Council Tax Reduction Schemes (Default Scheme) (Wales) Regulations 2013
Sch para 48 – Earnings of employed earners: persons who are not pensioners
Sub-para (1) amended by reg 22 of the Council Tax Reduction Schemes (Prescribed Requirements and Default Scheme) (Wales) (Amendment) Regulations 2015 SI No.44 (W.3) as from 21 January 2015 in relation to schemes made for financial years starting on or after 1 April 2015.

p1243 The Council Tax Reduction Schemes (Default Scheme) (Wales) Regulations 2013
Sch para 49 – Calculation of net earnings of employed earners: persons who are not pensioners
Sub-para (3) amended by reg 23 of the Council Tax Reduction Schemes (Prescribed Requirements and Default Scheme) (Wales) (Amendment) Regulations 2015 SI No.44 (W.3) as from 21 January 2015 in relation to schemes made for financial years starting on or after 1 April 2015.

pp1244-45 The Council Tax Reduction Schemes (Default Scheme) (Wales) Regulations 2013
Sch para 51 – Calculation of income other than earnings: persons who are not pensioners
Sub-para (4) amended by reg 24 of the Council Tax Reduction Schemes (Prescribed Requirements and Default Scheme) (Wales) (Amendment) Regulations 2015 SI No.44 (W.3) as from 21 January 2015 in relation to schemes made for financial years starting on or after 1 April 2015.

p1247-50 The Council Tax Reduction Schemes (Default Scheme) (Wales) Regulations 2013
Sch para 55 – Treatment of child care charges
Sub-paras (11), (15) and (16) amended by reg 25 of the Council Tax Reduction Schemes (Prescribed Requirements and Default Scheme) (Wales) (Amendment) Regulations 2015 SI No.44 (W.3) as from 21 January 2015 in relation to schemes made for financial years starting on or after 1 April 2015.

pp1259-61 The Council Tax Reduction Schemes (Default Scheme) (Wales) Regulations 2013
Sch para 70 – Interpretation
Definitions of "access funds" and "full-time course of study" amended by art 2 and Sch 3 para 31(3) of the Deregulation Act 2015 (Consequential Amendments) Order 2015 SI No.971 as from 26 May 2015.

In para 1, definitions of "cronfeydd mynediad" ("access funds") and "cwrs astudio amser llawn" ("full-time course of study") amended by art 2 and Sch 3 para 31(6) of the Deregulation Act 2015 (Consequential Amendments) Order 2015 SI No.971 as from 26 May 2015.

pp1282-83 The Council Tax Reduction Schemes (Default Scheme) (Wales) Regulations 2013
Sch para 72 – Students who are excluded from entitlement to council tax reduction under the scheme
Sub-para (2) amended by reg 26 of the Council Tax Reduction Schemes (Prescribed Requirements and Default Scheme) (Wales) (Amendment) Regulations 2015 SI No.44 (W.3) as from 21 January 2015 in relation to schemes made for financial years starting on or after 1 April 2015.

pp1281-84 The Council Tax Reduction Schemes (Default Scheme) (Wales) Regulations 2013
Sch 2 – Applicable amounts: pensioners
Amounts uprated by reg 27 of the Council Tax Reduction Schemes (Prescribed Requirements and Default Scheme) (Wales) (Amendment) Regulations 2015 SI No.44 (W.3) as from 21 January 2015 in relation to schemes made for financial years starting on or after 1 April 2015.

pp1284-93   The Council Tax Reduction Schemes (Default Scheme) (Wales) Regulations 2013 Sch 3 – Applicable amounts: persons who are not pensioners

Paras 18 and 23 to 26 amended and amounts uprated by reg 28 of the Council Tax Reduction Schemes (Prescribed Requirements and Default Scheme) (Wales) (Amendment) Regulations 2015 SI No.44 (W.3) as from 21 January 2015 in relation to schemes made for financial years starting on or after 1 April 2015.

pp1293-95   The Council Tax Reduction Schemes (Default Scheme) (Wales) Regulations 2013 Sch 4 – Sums disregarded from applicant's earnings: pensioners

Paras 5 and 6 amended by reg 29 of the Council Tax Reduction Schemes (Prescribed Requirements and Default Scheme) (Wales) (Amendment) Regulations 2015 SI No.44 (W.3) as from 21 January 2015 in relation to schemes made for financial years starting on or after 1 April 2015.

pp1298-1300   The Council Tax Reduction Schemes (Default Scheme) (Wales) Regulations 2013 Sch 6 – Sums disregarded in the calculation of earnings: persons who are not pensioners

Para 12 amended by reg 30 of the Council Tax Reduction Schemes (Prescribed Requirements and Default Scheme) (Wales) (Amendment) Regulations 2015 SI No.44 (W.3) as from 21 January 2015 in relation to schemes made for financial years starting on or after 1 April 2015.

pp1327-37   The Council Tax Reduction (Scotland) Regulations 2012 reg 2 – Interpretation

Definition of "couple" substituted by reg 3 of the Council Tax Reduction (Scotland) Amendment Regulations 2015 SSI No.46 as from 1 April 2015.

Definitions of "shared parental leave" and "statutory shared parental pay" inserted by art 23(2)(d) of the Shared Parental Leave and Statutory Shared Parental Pay (Consequential Amendments to Subordinate Legislation) Order 2014 SI No.3255 as from 31 December 2014. Definitions of "additional paternity leave" and "ordinary paternity leave" omitted and definition of "paternity leave" amended by art 23(2)(a)–(c) of that order as from 5 April 2015. Note: transitional provision is made under art 35.

Definitions of "full-time course of study" and "training allowance" amended by art 2 and Sch 3 para 18(2) of the Deregulation Act 2015 (Consequential Amendments) Order 2015 SI No.971 as from 26 May 2015.

pp1342-43   The Council Tax Reduction (Scotland) Regulations 2012 reg 6 – Remunerative work

Para (7) amended by art 23(3) of the Shared Parental Leave and Statutory Shared Parental Pay (Consequential Amendments to Subordinate Legislation) Order 2014 SI No.3255 as from 31 December 2014. Note: transitional provision is made under art 35.

pp1350-51   The Council Tax Reduction (Scotland) Regulations 2012 reg 16 – Persons not entitled to council tax reduction: persons treated as not being in Great Britain

Para (5)(e) substituted, para (5)(f) amended and paras (5)(h) and (i) inserted by reg 4 of the Council Tax Reduction (Scotland) Amendment Regulations 2015 SSI No.46 as from 1 April 2015.

pp1352-53   The Council Tax Reduction (Scotland) Regulations 2012 reg 19 – Persons not entitled to council tax reduction: persons subject to immigration control

The existing text becomes para (1), para (1) is then amended and para (2) inserted by reg 5 of the Council Tax Reduction (Scotland) Amendment Regulations 2015 SSI No.46 as from 1 April 2015.

pp1358-62   The Council Tax Reduction (Scotland) Regulations 2012 reg 28 – Treatment of child care charges

Paras (15) and (16) amended by art 23(4)(a)(i) and (iv) and (b)(i) and (iii) of the Shared Parental Leave and Statutory Shared Parental Pay (Consequential Amendments to Subordinate Legislation) Order 2014 SI No.3255 as from 31 December 2014. Paras (15) and (16) amended by art 23(4)(a)(ii) and (b)(ii) of that order as from 5 April 2015. Note: transitional provision is made under art 35.

pp1364-65   The Council Tax Reduction (Scotland) Regulations 2012 reg 34 – Earnings of employed earners

Para (1) amended by art 23(5)(b) of the Shared Parental Leave and Statutory Shared Parental Pay (Consequential Amendments to Subordinate Legislation) Order 2014 SI No.3255 as from 31 December 2014. Para (1) amended by art 23(5)(a) of that order as from 5 April 2015. Note: transitional provision is made under art 35.

pp1365-66   The Council Tax Reduction (Scotland) Regulations 2012 reg 35 – Calculation of net earnings of employed earners

Para (3) amended by reg 23(6)(b) of the Shared Parental Leave and Statutory Shared Parental Pay (Consequential Amendments to Subordinate Legislation) Order 2014 SI No.3255 as from 31 December 2014. Para (3) amended by reg 23(6)(a) of those regulations as from 5 April 2015. Note: transitional provision is made under reg 35 of those regulations.

pp1379-81   The Council Tax Reduction (Scotland) Regulations 2012 reg 52 – Interpretation: students

Definition of "access funds" amended by art 2 and Sch 3 para 18(3) of the Deregulation Act 2015 (Consequential Amendments) Order 2015 SI No.971 as from 26 May 2015.

pp1387-88   The Council Tax Reduction (Scotland) Regulations 2012 reg 67 – Non-dependant deductions

Amounts in para (1) uprated and para (7)(e) inserted by reg 6 of the Council Tax Reduction (Scotland) Amendment Regulations 2015 SSI No.46 as from 1 April 2015.

p1402   The Council Tax Reduction (Scotland) Regulations 2012 reg 90C – Panel to conduct further reviews

Para (1) amended by reg 7 of the Council Tax Reduction (Scotland) Amendment Regulations 2015 SSI No.46 as from 1 April 2015.

pp1402-03   The Council Tax Reduction (Scotland) Regulations 2012 reg 90D – Conduct of further reviews

Paras (5) and (6) amended and paras (6)(f), (6A), (6B) and (6C) inserted by reg 8 of the Council Tax Reduction (Scotland) Amendment Regulations 2015 SSI No.46 as from 1 April 2015.

pp1405-14   The Council Tax Reduction (Scotland) Regulations 2012 Sch 1 – Applicable amounts

Amounts uprated by reg 9 of the Council Tax Reduction (Scotland) Amendment Regulations 2015 SSI No.46 as from 1 April 2015.

pp1414-16   The Council Tax Reduction (Scotland) Regulations 2012 Sch 2 – Amount of alternative maximum council tax reduction

Amounts uprated by reg 10 of the Council Tax Reduction (Scotland) Amendment Regulations 2015 SSI No.46 as from 1 April 2015.

pp1416-18   The Council Tax Reduction (Scotland) Regulations 2012 Sch 3 – Sums to be disregarded in the calculation of earnings

Para 9(a) Substituted by reg 11 of the Council Tax Reduction (Scotland) Amendment Regulations 2015 SSI No.46 as from 1 April 2015.

pp1419-25   The Council Tax Reduction (Scotland) Regulations 2012 Sch 4 – Sums to be disregarded in the calculation of income other than earnings

New para 11A inserted by reg 13 of the Council Tax Reduction (Scotland) Amendment Regulations 2015 SSI No.46 as from 1 April 2015.

pp1426-32   The Council Tax Reduction (Scotland) Regulations 2012 Sch 5 – Capital to be disregarded

Paras 57 amended by reg 12 of the Council Tax Reduction (Scotland) Amendment Regulations 2015 SSI No.46 as from 1 April 2015.

pp1437-46 The Council Tax Reduction (State Pension Credit) (Scotland) Regulations 2012
reg 2 – Interpretation

Definition of "couple" substituted by reg 15 of the Council Tax Reduction (Scotland) Amendment Regulations 2015 SSI No.46 as from 1 April 2015.

Definitions of "shared parental leave" and "statutory shared parental pay" inserted by art 24(2)(d)(i) and (iii) of the Shared Parental Leave and Statutory Shared Parental Pay (Consequential Amendments to Subordinate Legislation) Order 2014 SI No.3255 as from 31 December 2014. Definitions of "additional paternity leave" and "ordinary paternity leave" omitted, definition of "paternity leave" amended and definition of "statutory paternity pay" inserted by art 24(2)(a)–(c) and (d)(ii) of that order as from 5 April 2015. Note: transitional provision is made under art 35.

Definition of "training allowance" amended by art 2 and Sch 3 para 19 of the Deregulation Act 2015 (Consequential Amendments) Order 2015 SI No.971 as from 26 May 2015.

p1451 The Council Tax Reduction (State Pension Credit) (Scotland) Regulations 2012
reg 6 – Remunerative work

Para (7) amended by art 24(3) of the Shared Parental Leave and Statutory Shared Parental Pay (Consequential Amendments to Subordinate Legislation) Order 2014 SI No.3255 as from 31 December 2014. Note: transitional provision is made under art 35.

p1456 The Council Tax Reduction (State Pension Credit) (Scotland) Regulations 2012
reg 16 – Persons not entitled to council tax reduction: persons treated as not in Great Britain

Para (5)(e) substituted and para (5)(h) and (i) inserted by reg 15 of the Council Tax Reduction (Scotland) Amendment Regulations 2015 SSI No.46 as from 1 April 2015.

p1458 The Council Tax Reduction (State Pension Credit) (Scotland) Regulations 2012
reg 19 – Persons not entitled to council tax reduction: persons subject to immigration control

The existing text becomes para (1), para (1) is then amended and para (2) inserted by reg 17 of the Council Tax Reduction (Scotland) Amendment Regulations 2015 SSI No.46 as from 1 April 2015.

pp1461-63 The Council Tax Reduction (State Pension Credit) (Scotland) Regulations 2012
reg 27 – meaning of "income"

Para (1) amended by art 24(4)(b) of the Shared Parental Leave and Statutory Shared Parental Pay (Consequential Amendments to Subordinate Legislation) Order 2014 SI No.3255 as from 31 December 2014. Para (1) amended by art 24(4)(a) of that order as from 5 April 2015. Note: transitional provision is made under art 35.

pp1463-67 The Council Tax Reduction (State Pension Credit) (Scotland) Regulations 2012
reg 29 – treatment of child care charges

Paras (15) and (16) amended by art 24(5)(a)(i) and (iv) and (b)(i) and (iv) of the Shared Parental Leave and Statutory Shared Parental Pay (Consequential Amendments to Subordinate Legislation) Order 2014 SI No.3255 as from 31 December 2014. Paras (15) and (16) amended by art 24(5)(a)(ii) and (iii) and (b)(ii) and (iii) of those regulations as from 5 April 2015. Note: transitional provision is made under art 35.

pp1469-70 The Council Tax Reduction (State Pension Credit) (Scotland) Regulations 2012
reg 32 – Earnings of employed earners

Para (1) amended by art 24(6)(b) of the Shared Parental Leave and Statutory Shared Parental Pay (Consequential Amendments to Subordinate Legislation) Order 2014 SI No.3255 as from 31 December 2014. Para (1) amended by art 24(6)(a) of those regulations as from 5 April 2015. Note: transitional provision is made under art 35.

pp1470-71 The Council Tax Reduction (State Pension Credit) (Scotland) Regulations 2012
reg 33 – Calculation of net earnings of employed earners

Para (2) amended by art 24(7)(c) of the Shared Parental Leave and Statutory Shared Parental Pay (Consequential Amendments to Subordinate Legislation) Order 2014 SI No.3255 as from 31

December 2014. Para (2) amended by art 24(7)(a) and (b) of those regulations as from 5 April 2015. Note: transitional provision is made under art 35.

pp1481-82 **The Council Tax Reduction (State Pension Credit) (Scotland) Regulations 2012 reg 48 – Non-dependant deductions**
Amounts uprated and para (7)(e) inserted by reg 18 of the Council Tax Reduction (Scotland) Amendment Regulations 2015 SSI No.46 as from 1 April 2015.

p1496 **The Council Tax Reduction (State Pension Credit) (Scotland) Regulations 2012 reg 70C – Conduct of further reviews**
Paras (5) and (6)(a) amended and para (6)(f), (6A), (6B) and (6C) inserted by reg 19 of the Council Tax Reduction (Scotland) Amendment Regulations 2015 SSI No.46 as from 1 April 2015.

pp1498-1502 **The Council Tax Reduction (State Pension Credit) (Scotland) Regulations 2012 Sch 1 – Applicable amounts**
Amounts uprated by reg 20 of the Council Tax Reduction (Scotland) Amendment Regulations 2015 SSI No.46 as from 1 April 2015.

pp1502-05 **The Council Tax Reduction (State Pension Credit) (Scotland) Regulations 2012 Sch 2 – Sums to be disregarded in the calculation of earnings**
Para 3(2)(b) substituted by reg 21 of the Council Tax Reduction (Scotland) Amendment Regulations 2015 SSI No.46 as from 1 April 2015.

pp1507-11 **The Council Tax Reduction (State Pension Credit) (Scotland) Regulations 2012 Sch 4 – Capital disregards**
Paras 21(2)(o) and 22(2)(e) inserted and para 29 amended by reg 22 of the Council Tax Reduction (Scotland) Amendment Regulations 2015 SSI No.46 as from 1 April 2015.

pp1512-13 **The Council Tax Reduction (State Pension Credit) (Scotland) Regulations 2012 Sch 5 – Amount of alternative maximum council tax reduction**
Amounts uprated by reg 23 of the Council Tax Reduction (Scotland) Amendment Regulations 2015 SSI No.46 as from 1 April 2015.

p1599 **The Discretionary Financial Assistance Regulations 2001**
[p1599: In the General Note to the regulations, after the second paragraph, add:]

DHPs are now seen to be a part of the package for dealing with the problems for claimants of under-occupation of accommodation and its impact on the amount of HB to which they are entitled – ie, DHPs are meant to "plug the gap": see, for example, *R (MA and Others) v SSWP and Birmingham City Council* [2014] EWCA Civ 13, 21 February 2014. The government has allocated extra funding for this purpose and has provided additional guidance in a good practice guide. See the Analysis of reg 2(2) on the amount of a DHP.

pp1599-1601 **The Discretionary Financial Assistance Regulations 2001 reg 2 – Discretionary housing payments**
[p1600: In the Analysis of para (2), after the first paragraph, add:]

In *R (Hardy) v Sandwell MBC* [2015] EWHC 890 (Admin), 30 March 2015, the High Court considered whether a local authority could take DLA care component into account in determining the amount of a DHP. Mr Hardy's HB entitlement had been reduced under reg B13 HB Regs for underoccupying his accommodation. He and his wife were both disabled and in receipt of DLA. The local authority awarded DHPs to plug the gap. In so doing, it disregarded the couple's DLA mobility component, but took the care component fully into account. This decision was successfully challenged on a number of grounds.
(1) The local authority's policy was contrary to the DWP's *DHP Guidance Manual and Good Practice Guide* and was an unlawful fetter on the council's discretion. Mr Justice Phillips decided that the local authority's blanket policy of always taking DLA care component into

account and ignoring only DLA mobility component was based on a misunderstanding of its powers – ie, that it adopted its policy to take DLA care component into account because it incorrectly understood that it was not allowed to exclude it. The local authority, therefore, had not given proper consideration to the *DHP Guidance and Good Practice Guide* and had not exercised its discretion on the issue properly or at all.

(2) Taking DLA care component into account in determining the amount of a DHP constituted unlawful discrimination arising from disability contrary to Article 14 of the European Convention on Human Rights. Mr Justice Phillips considered DHPs in the context of the HB scheme as a whole, in particular because it had been established that, unless the availability of DHPs is taken into account, reg B13 HB Regs discriminates against disabled HB claimants (see pp354–46 for commentary on the caselaw and in particular on *R (MA and Others) v SSWP and Birmingham City Council* [2014] EWCA Civ 13, 21 February 2014). He decided that DHPs come within the ambit of Article 1 Protocol 1, and Article 14 is engaged in decisions whether to award a DHP to a disabled claimant. The judge also said that awards of DHPs to disabled applicants are sufficiently related to their Article 8 rights that Article 14 is also engaged in that regard. He said:

> "52. ...the Government has provided additional funding for DHPs for the very purpose of ensuring that disabled persons affected by the HB size criteria are not forced to leave their accommodation (where that would otherwise be the avowed purpose of the reduction in HB), not least because it is recognised that the accommodation may well have been adapted to meet their disability needs. It is therefore plain that DHPs are provided to protect the private and family life of disabled applicants, in particular their recognised need to keep their existing home. Further, the decision of a local authority as to whether to reduce such DHPs below the shortfall in rent directly impacts on those interests."

In his judgment, the local authority's' approach amounted to indirect discrimination against the claimant on grounds of disability. Because the discriminatory effect of the HB size criteria could only be justified by the availability of DHPs to make up any shortfall, and additional government funding had been provided to local authorities for this purpose, the discrimination could not be justified. Agreeing with *R (MA)* he said that local authorities were acting wrongly by including DLA care component in household income when determining the amount of DHPs.

pp1671-72   The Social Security (Information Sharing in Relation to Welfare Services etc) Regulations 2012 reg 2 – Interpretation

Definition of "social landlord" substituted and definitions of "universal credit claimant" and "universal support initiative" inserted by reg 2(2) of the Social Security (Information-sharing in relation to Welfare Services etc) (Amendment) Regulations 2015 SI No.46 as from 13 February 2015.

pp1673-74   The Social Security (Information Sharing in Relation to Welfare Services etc) Regulations 2012 reg 5 – Supply of relevant information by the Secretary of State

Paras (1)(g) and (h), (3A) and (4)(e) inserted by reg 2(3) of the Social Security (Information-sharing in relation to Welfare Services etc) (Amendment) Regulations 2015 SI No.46 as from 13 February 2015.

pp1674-76   The Social Security (Information Sharing in Relation to Welfare Services etc) Regulations 2012 reg 6 – Holding purposes

Para (1)(q) inserted by reg 2(4) of the Social Security (Information-sharing in relation to Welfare Services etc) (Amendment) Regulations 2015 SI No.46 as from 13 February 2015.

p1678   The Social Security (Information Sharing in Relation to Welfare Services etc) Regulations 2012 new reg 9C – Using purposes connected with a universal support initiative

New reg 9C inserted by reg 2(5) of the Social Security (Information-sharing in relation to Welfare Services etc) (Amendment) Regulations 2015 SI No.46 as from 13 February 2015.

p1678   **The Social Security (Information Sharing in Relation to Welfare Services etc) Regulations 2012 reg 10 – Qualifying persons**

Para (1) amended by reg 2(6) of the Social Security (Information-sharing in relation to Welfare Services etc) (Amendment) Regulations 2015 SI No.46 as from 13 February 2015.

p1680   **The Social Security (Information Sharing in Relation to Welfare Services etc) Regulations 2012 reg 16 – Holding purposes**

Para (d) inserted by reg 2(7) of the Social Security (Information-sharing in relation to Welfare Services etc) (Amendment) Regulations 2015 SI No.46 as from 13 February 2015.

p1680   **The Social Security (Information Sharing in Relation to Welfare Services etc) Regulations 2012 reg 17 – Prescribed purposes relating to relevant social security benefit**

Para (3) amended by reg 2(8) of the Social Security (Information-sharing in relation to Welfare Services etc) (Amendment) Regulations 2015 SI No.46 as from 13 February 2015.

PART II:

PRIMARY LEGISLATION

Further amendments

126.–(1)–(2) *[Omitted]*

(3)   A reference to statutory paternity pay in an enactment (including an enactment amended by this Act) or in an instrument or document is to be read, in relation to any time that falls–

(a)   after the commencement of paragraphs 12 and 13 of Schedule 1 to the Work and Families Act 2006, and

(b)   before the commencement of paragraphs 12 and 13 of Schedule 7, as a reference to ordinary statutory paternity pay.

(4)   Subsection (3) does not apply to the extent that a reference to statutory paternity pay is a reference to additional statutory paternity pay.

Commencement

5.4.15.

SCHEDULE 7

Section 126

STATUTORY RIGHTS TO LEAVE AND PAY: FURTHER AMENDMENTS

Social Security Contributions and Benefits Act 1992 (c. 4)

12.–(1)   Section 171ZA (entitlement to ordinary statutory paternity pay: birth) is amended as follows.

(2)   In subsection (1), for ''ordinary statutory paternity pay'' there is substituted ''statutory paternity pay''.

(3)   In subsection (4), the word "ordinary" is repealed.

13.–(1)   Section 171ZB (entitlement to ordinary statutory paternity pay: adoption) is amended as follows.

(2)   In subsection (1), for ''ordinary statutory paternity pay'' there is substituted ''statutory paternity pay''.

(3)   In subsection (4), the word "ordinary" is repealed.

(4)   In subsection (6), the word "ordinary" is repealed.

Commencement

5.4.15.

PART III:

SECONDARY LEGISLATION

The Children and Families Act 2014 (Commencement No.3, Transitional Provisions and Savings) Order 2014

(SI 2014 No.1640)

Made   26th June 2014

The Secretary of State, in exercise of the powers conferred by sections 137(1) and 139(6) of the Children and Families Act 2014, makes the following Order.

Citation

1. This Order may be cited as the Children and Families Act 2014 (Commencement No. 3, Transitional Provisions and Savings) Order 2014.

Interpretation

2. In this Order–
"the 1992 Act" means the Social Security Contributions and Benefits Act 1992;
"the 2014 Act" means the Children and Families Act 2014; and
"expected week of birth" means the week, beginning with midnight between Saturday and Sunday, in which it is expected that a child will be born.

Provisions coming into force on 5th April 2015

6. The following provisions of Parts 7 and 8 of the 2014 Act come into force on 5th April 2015 subject to the transitional and saving provisions in articles 13 to 15–
(a)-(b) *[Omitted]*
(c) section 126(1) (in so far as it relates to the provisions listed in article 7), (2) to (4) (further amendments);
(d)-(e) *[Omitted]*

7. The following provisions of Schedule 7 to the 2014 Act come into force on 5th April 2015 subject to the transitional and saving provisions in articles 16, 17, and 19–
(a)-(f) *[Omitted]*
(g) paragraphs 10 to 22;
(h)-(pp) *[Omitted]*

Transitional and saving provisions for provisions coming into force on 5th April 2015

15. Section 126(2) to (4) (further amendments) of the 2014 Act does not have effect in relation to–
(a) children whose expected week of birth ends on or before 4th April 2015;
(b) children placed for adoption on or before 4th April 2015.

16. The amendments and repeals made by the provisions of Schedule 7 to the Act listed in article 7 do not have effect in relation to–
(a) children whose expected week of birth ends on or before 4th April 2015;
(b) children placed for adoption on or before 4th April 2015.

The Welfare Reform Act 2012 (Commencement No.20 and Transitional and Transitory Provisions and Commencement No.9 and Transitional and Transitory Provisions (Amendment)) Order 2014

(SI 2014 No.3094)

Made   21st November 2014

The Secretary of State for Work and Pensions makes the following Order in exercise of the powers conferred by sections 150(3) and (4)(a), (b)(i) and (c) of the Welfare Reform Act 2012:

Citation, commencement and interpretation

1.   This Order may be cited as the Welfare Reform Act 2012 (Commencement No. 20 and Transitional and Transitory Provisions and Commencement No. 9 and Transitional and Transitory Provisions (Amendment)) Order 2014.

Interpretation

2.–(1)   In this Order–

"housing benefit" means housing benefit under section 130 of the Social Security Contributions and Benefits Act 1992;

"the No. 9 Order" means the Welfare Reform Act 2012 (Commencement No. 9 and Transitional and Transitory Provisions and Commencement No. 8 and Savings and Transitional Provisions (Amendment)) Order 2013;

"the No. 28 relevant district" means the postcode part-district SM5 2;

Transitional provision: claims for housing benefit, income support or a tax credit

6.–(1)   Except as provided by paragraphs (2) to (5) and (8), a person may not make a claim for housing benefit, income support or a tax credit (in the latter case, whether or not as part of a Tax Credits Act couple) on any date where, if that person made a claim for universal credit on that date (whether or not as part of a couple), the provisions of the Act listed in Schedule 2 to the No. 9 Order would come into force under article 3(1) and (2)(a) of this Order in relation to that claim for universal credit.

(2)   Paragraph (1) does not apply to a claim for housing benefit in respect of specified accommodation.

(3)   Paragraph (1) does not apply to a claim for housing benefit or a tax credit where–

(a)   in the case of a claim for housing benefit, the claim is made by a person who has reached the qualifying age for state pension credit, or by a person who is a member of a State Pension Credit Act couple the other member of which has reached that age;

(b)   *[Omitted]*

(4)-(6)   *[Omitted]*

(7)   For the purposes of this article–

(a)   a person makes a claim for income support, housing benefit or a tax credit if the person takes any action which results in a decision on a claim being required under the relevant Regulations; and

(b)   except as provided in paragraph (8), it is irrelevant that the effect of any provision of the relevant Regulations is that, for the purpose of those Regulations, the claim is made or treated as made on a date that is earlier than the date on which that action was taken.

(8)   Paragraph (1) does not apply to a claim for housing benefit or income support where–

(a)   in the case of a claim for housing benefit–

(i)   first notification of the person's intention to make the claim is given (within the meaning of regulation 83(5)(d) of the Housing Benefit

Regulations 2006 ("the 2006 Regulations") or, as the case may be, regulation 64(6)(d) of the Housing Benefit (Persons who have attained the qualifying age for state pension credit) Regulations 2006 ("the 2006 (SPC) Regulations")) before 26th November 2014; or

    (ii)   a defective claim for housing benefit (within the meaning of the 2006 Regulations or the 2006 (SPC) Regulations) is made before 26th November 2014 and it is corrected or completed on or after that date;

(b)   *[Omitted]*

(9)-(10)   *[Omitted]*

(11)   For the purposes of this article–

(a)   "couple" (apart from in the expressions "State Pension Credit Act couple" and "Tax Credit Act couple"), has the meaning given in section 39 of the Act;

(b)   "qualifying age for state pension credit" means the qualifying age referred to in section 1(6) of the State Pension Credit Act 2002;

(c)   the "relevant Regulations" means–

    (i)   *[Omitted]*

    (ii)   in the case of a claim for housing benefit, the 2006 Regulations or, as the case may be, the 2006 (SPC) Regulations;

    (iii)   *[Omitted]*

(d)   "specified accommodation" means accommodation to which one or more of subparagraphs (2) to (5) of paragraph 3A of Schedule 1 to the Universal Credit Regulations 2013 applies;

(e)   "State Pension Credit Act couple" means a couple as defined in section 17 of the State Pension Credit Act 2002;

(f)   *[Omitted]*

The Jobseeker's Allowance (18–21 Work Skills Pilot Scheme) Regulations 2014

(SI 2014 No.3117)

Made   *24th November 2014*
Coming into force in accordance with regulation 1(1)

The Secretary of State for Work and Pensions makes the following Regulations in exercise of the powers conferred by sections 123(1)(d), 136(5)(a) and (b), 137(1) and 175(1), (3), (4) and (6) of the Social Security Contributions and Benefits Act 1992, sections 12(4)(a) and (b), 17A(1), (2), (5)(a) and (b), 20E(3)(a), 29, 35(1) and 36(2), (4) and (4A) of the Jobseekers Act 1995 and sections 30 and 146(1) and (2) of the Housing Grants, Construction and Regeneration Act 1996.

These Regulations are made with a view to ascertaining whether their provisions will, or will be likely to, encourage persons to obtain or remain in work or will, or will be likely to, make it more likely that persons will obtain or remain in work or be able to do so.

These Regulations are made with the consent of the Treasury in respect of provisions relating to section 30(e) of the Housing Grants, Construction and Regeneration Act 1996.

In respect of provisions in these Regulations relating to housing benefit, organisations appearing to the Secretary of State to be representative of the authorities concerned have agreed that consultations need not be undertaken.

The Social Security Advisory Committee has agreed that the proposals in respect of these Regulations should not be referred to it.

A draft of this instrument was laid before Parliament in accordance with section 37(2) of the Jobseekers Act 1995 and approved by a resolution of each House of Parliament.

Citation, commencement and duration

1.–(1) These Regulations may be cited as the Jobseeker's Allowance (18-21 Work Skills Pilot Scheme) Regulations 2014 and come into force on the day after the day on which they are made.

(2) They cease to have effect at the end of the period of 24 months beginning with the day on which they come into force.

Interpretation

2.–(1) In these Regulations–
"the Housing Benefit Regulations" means the Housing Benefit Regulations 2006;
"pilot area" means a Jobcentre Plus district of the Department for Work and Pensions, by whatever name it is from time to time known, which is identified by reference to its name at the date these Regulations come into force as listed below–
    (a)   Black Country;
    (b)   Devon, Somerset and Cornwall;
    (c)   Kent;
    (d)   Mercia;

Notional income

15.–(1) This regulation applies to the following provisions (which relate to notional income)–
    (a)   regulation 42(7) of the Housing Benefit Regulations;
    (b)-(c) *[Omitted]*

(2) In each of the provisions to which this regulation applies, after sub-paragraph (cd) insert–

    "(ce) in respect of a person's participation in a scheme prescribed in regulation 3 of the Jobseekers Allowance (18 – 21 Work Skills Pilot Scheme) Regulations 2014;"

Notional capital

16.–(1)   This regulation applies to the following provisions (which relate to notional capital)–

(a)   regulation 49(4) of the Housing Benefit Regulations;

(b)-(c) *[Omitted]*

(2)   In each of the provisions to which this regulation applies, after sub-paragraph (bd) insert–

"(be)   in respect of a person's participation in a scheme prescribed in regulation 3 of the Jobseekers Allowance (18 – 21 Work Skills Pilot Scheme) Regulations 2014;".

Income to be disregarded

17.–(1)   This regulation applies to the following Schedules (which relate to sums to be disregarded in the calculation of income other than earnings)–

(a)   Schedule 5 to the Housing Benefit Regulations;

(b)-(c) *[Omitted]*

(2)   In each of the Schedules to which this regulation applies, after paragraph A4 insert–

"**A5.**   Any payment made to the claimant in respect of any child care, travel or other expenses incurred, or to be incurred, by the claimant in respect of their participation in a scheme prescribed in regulation 3 of the Jobseekers Allowance (18 – 21 Work Skills Pilot Scheme) Regulations 2014.".

Capital to be disregarded

18.–(1)   This regulation applies to the following Schedules (which relate to capital to be disregarded)–

(a)   Schedule 6 to the Housing Benefit Regulations;

(b)-(c) *[Omitted]*

(2)   In each of the Schedules to which this regulation applies, after paragraph A4 insert–

"**A5.**   Any payment made to the claimant in respect of any child care, travel or other expenses incurred, or to be incurred, by the claimant in respect of their participation in a scheme prescribed in regulation 3 of the Jobseekers Allowance (18 – 21 Work Skills Pilot Scheme) Regulations 2014, but only for 52 weeks beginning with the date of receipt of the payment.".

The Rent Officers (Housing benefit and Universal Credit Functions) (Local Housing Allowance Amendments) Order 2014

(SI 2014 No.3126)

Made	*24th November 2014*
Laid before Parliament	*1st December 2014*
Coming into force	*8th January 2015*

The Secretary of State for Work and Pensions makes the following Order in exercise of the powers conferred by section 122(1) and (6) of the Housing Act 1996.

Citation and commencement

1. This Order may be cited as the Rent Officers (Housing Benefit and Universal Credit Functions) (Local Housing Allowance Amendments) Order 2014 and comes into force on 8th January 2015.

Amendment to the Rent Officers (Housing Benefit Functions) Order 1997

2.–(1) The Rent Officers (Housing Benefit Functions) Order 1997 is amended as follows.

(2) For paragraph (2B) of article 4B (broad rental market area determinations and local housing allowance determinations) substitute–

"(2B) The date specified for the purposes of paragraph (2A) is the last working day of January.".

(3) Schedule 3B (broad rental market area determinations and local housing allowance determinations) is amended as follows–

(a) For the table in sub-paragraph (9) of paragraph 2 (local housing allowance for category of dwelling in paragraph 1)(e) substitute–

(1) Paragraph of this Schedule defining the category of dwelling	*(2) Maximum local housing allowance for that category of dwelling*
paragraph 1(1)(a) (one bedroom, shared accommodation)	£260.64
paragraph 1(1)(b) (one bedroom, exclusive use)	£260.64
paragraph 1(1)(c) (two bedrooms)	£302.33
paragraph 1(1)(d) (three bedrooms)	£354.46
paragraph 1(1)(e) (four bedrooms)	£417.02."

(b) For the table in paragraph 6 substitute the table in Schedule 1 to this Order.

Amendment to the Rent Officers (Housing Benefit Functions) (Scotland) Order 1997

3.–(1) The Rent Officers (Housing Benefit Functions) (Scotland) Order 1997 is amended as follows.

(2) For paragraph (2B) of article 4B (broad rental market area determinations and local housing allowance determinations) substitute–

"(2B) The date specified for the purposes of paragraph (2A) is the last working day of January.".

(3) Schedule 3B (broad rental market area determinations and local housing allowance determinations) is amended as follows–

(a)   For the table in sub-paragraph (9) of paragraph 2 (local housing allowance for category of dwelling in paragraph 1) substitute–

"(1) Paragraph of this Schedule defining the category of dwelling	*(2) Maximum local housing allowance for that category of dwelling*
paragraph 1(1)(a) (one bedroom, shared accommodation)	£260.64
paragraph 1(1)(b) (one bedroom, exclusive use)	£260.64
paragraph 1(1)(c) (two bedrooms)	£302.33
paragraph 1(1)(d) (three bedrooms)	£354.46
paragraph 1(1)(e) (four bedrooms)	£417.02."

(b)   For the table in paragraph 6 substitute the table in Schedule 2 to this Order.

SCHEDULE 1
Article 2(3)(b)

Table to be substituted for the table in paragraph 6 of Schedule 3B to the Rent Officers (Housing Benefit Functions) Order 1997

"(1) Broad rental market area	*(2) Paragraph of this Schedule defining the category of dwelling*
Ashford	Paragraph 1(1)(c)(two bedrooms)
	Paragraph 1(1)(d)(three bedrooms)
Aylesbury	Paragraph 1(1)(d)(three bedrooms)
Barnsley	Paragraph 1(1)(d)(three bedrooms)
Barrow-in-Furness	Paragraph 1(1)(b)(one bedroom, exclusive use)
Basingstoke	Paragraph 1(1)(a)(one bedroom, shared accommodation)
	Paragraph 1(1)(e)(four bedrooms)
Bedford	Paragraph 1(1)(c)(two bedrooms)
Birmingham	Paragraph 1(1)(d)(three bedrooms)
	Paragraph 1(1)(e)(four bedrooms)
Blackwater Valley	Paragraph 1(1)(a)(one bedroom, shared accommodation)
	Paragraph 1(1)(e)(four bedrooms)
Blaenau Gwent	Paragraph 1(1)(a)(one bedroom, shared accommodation)
	Paragraph 1(1)(b)(one bedroom, exclusive use)
Bolton and Bury	Paragraph 1(1)(a)(one bedroom, shared accommodation)
	Paragraph 1(1)(b)(one bedroom, exclusive use)
Brighton and Hove	Paragraph 1(1)(a)(one bedroom, shared accommodation)
	Paragraph 1(1)(e)(four bedrooms)
Bristol	Paragraph 1(1)(b)(one bedroom, exclusive use)
	Paragraph 1(1)(c)(two bedrooms)
	Paragraph 1(1)(e)(four bedrooms)
	Paragraph 1(1)(d)(three bedrooms)
Bury St Edmunds	Paragraph 1(1)(e)(four bedrooms)
Canterbury	Paragraph 1(1)(b)(one bedroom, exclusive use)
	Paragraph 1(1)(c)(two bedrooms)
	Paragraph 1(1)(e)(four bedrooms)
Central Greater Manchester	Paragraph 1(1)(a)(one bedroom, shared accommodation)
	Paragraph 1(1)(b)(one bedroom, exclusive use)
	Paragraph 1(1)(c)(two bedrooms)
	Paragraph 1(1)(d)(three bedrooms)
Central London	Paragraph 1(1)(a)(one bedroom, shared accommodation)
Central Norfolk & Norwich	Paragraph 1(1)(a)(one bedroom, shared accommodation)
Ceredigion	Paragraph 1(1)(c)(two bedrooms)
Chelmsford	Paragraph 1(1)(b)(one bedroom, exclusive use)
Cherwell Valley	Paragraph 1(1)(a)(one bedroom, shared accommodation)
	Paragraph 1(1)(b)(one bedroom, exclusive use)
	Paragraph 1(1)(d)(three bedrooms)
	Paragraph 1(1)(e)(four bedrooms)
Chichester	Paragraph 1(1)(c)(two bedrooms)
Chilterns	Paragraph 1(1)(b)(one bedroom, exclusive use)
	Paragraph 1(1)(d)(three bedrooms)
Crawley & Reigate	Paragraph 1(1)(b)(one bedroom, exclusive use)
	Paragraph 1(1)(c)(two bedrooms)

Darlington	Paragraph 1(1)(a)(one bedroom, shared accommodation)
Doncaster	Paragraph 1(1)(a)(one bedroom, shared accommodation)
Dover-Shepway	Paragraph 1(1)(e)(four bedrooms)
East Cheshire	Paragraph 1(1)(d)(three bedrooms)
	Paragraph 1(1)(e)(four bedrooms)
East Lancs	Paragraph 1(1)(e)(four bedrooms)
East Thames Valley	Paragraph 1(1)(d)(three bedrooms)
	Paragraph 1(1)(e)(four bedrooms)
Eastbourne	Paragraph 1(1)(e)(four bedrooms)
Eastern Staffordshire	Paragraph 1(1)(a)(one bedroom, shared accommodation)
Fylde Coast	Paragraph 1(1)(a)(one bedroom, shared accommodation)
Grantham & Newark	Paragraph 1(1)(a)(one bedroom, shared accommodation)
	Paragraph 1(1)(e)(four bedrooms)
Greater Liverpool	Paragraph 1(1)(a)(one bedroom, shared accommodation)
	Paragraph 1(1)(e)(four bedrooms)
Guildford	Paragraph 1(1)(a)(one bedroom, shared accommodation)
	Paragraph 1(1)(c)(two bedrooms)
Harlow & Stortford	Paragraph 1(1)(b)(one bedroom, exclusive use)
Herefordshire	Paragraph 1(1)(a)(one bedroom, shared accommodation)
High Weald	Paragraph 1(1)(d)(three bedrooms)
Hull & East Riding	Paragraph 1(1)(a)(one bedroom, shared accommodation)
Huntingdon	Paragraph 1(1)(c)(two bedrooms)
	Paragraph 1(1)(d)(three bedrooms)
Inner East London	Paragraph 1(1)(a)(one bedroom, shared accommodation)
Inner North London	Paragraph 1(1)(a)(one bedroom, shared accommodation)
Inner South East London	Paragraph 1(1)(a)(one bedroom, shared accommodation)
	Paragraph 1(1)(b)(one bedroom, exclusive use)
	Paragraph 1(1)(c)(two bedrooms)
	Paragraph 1(1)(d)(three bedrooms)
Inner South West London	Paragraph 1(1)(a)(one bedroom, shared accommodation)
	Paragraph 1(1)(b)(one bedroom, exclusive use)
Inner West London	Paragraph 1(1)(a)(one bedroom, shared accommodation)
	Paragraph 1(1)(b)(one bedroom, exclusive use)
Kings Lynn	Paragraph 1(1)(a)(one bedroom, shared accommodation)
Lancaster	Paragraph 1(1)(a)(one bedroom, shared accommodation)
	Paragraph 1(1)(e)(four bedrooms)
Luton	Paragraph 1(1)(a)(one bedroom, shared accommodation)
Maidstone	Paragraph 1(1)(c)(two bedrooms)
Medway & Swale	Paragraph 1(1)(a)(one bedroom, shared accommodation)
Merthyr Cynon	Paragraph 1(1)(a)(one bedroom, shared accommodation)
	Paragraph 1(1)(e)(four bedrooms)
Milton Keynes	Paragraph 1(1)(b)(one bedroom, exclusive use)
	Paragraph 1(1)(c)(two bedrooms)
Monmouthshire	Paragraph 1(1)(a)(one bedroom, shared accommodation)
Neath Port Talbot	Paragraph 1(1)(a)(one bedroom, shared accommodation)
Newbury	Paragraph 1(1)(a)(one bedroom, shared accommodation)
	Paragraph 1(1)(e)(four bedrooms)
Newport	Paragraph 1(1)(a)(one bedroom, shared accommodation)
North Clwyd	Paragraph 1(1)(a)(one bedroom, shared accommodation)
North Cornwall & Devon Borders	Paragraph 1(1)(e)(four bedrooms)
North Devon	Paragraph 1(1)(e)(four bedrooms)
North Nottingham	Paragraph 1(1)(a)(one bedroom, shared accommodation)
	Paragraph 1(1)(e)(four bedrooms)
North West Kent	Paragraph 1(1)(a)(one bedroom, shared accommodation)
	Paragraph 1(1)(e)(four bedrooms)
North West London	Paragraph 1(1)(a)(one bedroom, shared accommodation)
	Paragraph 1(1)(c)(two bedrooms)
	Paragraph 1(1)(e)(four bedrooms)
Northampton	Paragraph 1(1)(a)(one bedroom, shared accommodation)
Outer East London	Paragraph 1(1)(a)(one bedroom, shared accommodation)
	Paragraph 1(1)(c)(two bedrooms)
	Paragraph 1(1)(d)(three bedrooms)
	Paragraph 1(1)(e)(four bedrooms)
Outer North East London	Paragraph 1(1)(a)(one bedroom, shared accommodation)
	Paragraph 1(1)(d)(three bedrooms)
Outer North London	Paragraph 1(1)(a)(one bedroom, shared accommodation)
	Paragraph 1(1)(b)(one bedroom, exclusive use)

	Paragraph 1(1)(c)(two bedrooms)
	Paragraph 1(1)(d)(three bedrooms)
Outer South East London	Paragraph 1(1)(a)(one bedroom, shared accommodation)
	Paragraph 1(1)(b)(one bedroom, exclusive use)
	Paragraph 1(1)(d)(three bedrooms)
Outer South London	Paragraph 1(1)(a)(one bedroom, shared accommodation)
	Paragraph 1(1)(b)(one bedroom, exclusive use)
	Paragraph 1(1)(c)(two bedrooms)
	Paragraph 1(1)(d)(three bedrooms)
	Paragraph 1(1)(e)(four bedrooms)
Outer South West London	Paragraph 1(1)(a)(one bedroom, shared accommodation)
	Paragraph 1(1)(c)(two bedrooms)
	Paragraph 1(1)(d)(three bedrooms)
	Paragraph 1(1)(e)(four bedrooms)
Outer West London	Paragraph 1(1)(a)(one bedroom, shared accommodation)
	Paragraph 1(1)(b)(one bedroom, exclusive use)
	Paragraph 1(1)(c)(two bedrooms)
	Paragraph 1(1)(d)(three bedrooms)
	Paragraph 1(1)(e)(four bedrooms)
Peaks & Dales	Paragraph 1(1)(e)(four bedrooms)
Plymouth	Paragraph 1(1)(d)(three bedrooms)
Portsmouth	Paragraph 1(1)(e)(four bedrooms)
Reading	Paragraph 1(1)(a)(one bedroom, shared accommodation)
	Paragraph 1(1)(d)(three bedrooms)
	Paragraph 1(1)(e)(four bedrooms)
Scarborough	Paragraph 1(1)(a)(one bedroom, shared accommodation)
Sheffield	Paragraph 1(1)(b)(one bedroom, exclusive use)
	Paragraph 1(1)(e)(four bedrooms)
South Cheshire	Paragraph 1(1)(a)(one bedroom, shared accommodation)
South East Herts	Paragraph 1(1)(d)(three bedrooms)
South West Essex	Paragraph 1(1)(e)(four bedrooms)
South West Herts	Paragraph 1(1)(b)(one bedroom, exclusive use)
	Paragraph 1(1)(c)(two bedrooms)
	Paragraph 1(1)(d)(three bedrooms)
	Paragraph 1(1)(e)(four bedrooms)
Southampton	Paragraph 1(1)(e)(four bedrooms)
Southend	Paragraph 1(1)(e)(four bedrooms)
Southern Greater Manchester	Paragraph 1(1)(a)(one bedroom, shared accommodation)
	Paragraph 1(1)(d)(three bedrooms)
Southport	Paragraph 1(1)(a)(one bedroom, shared accommodation)
Staffordshire North	Paragraph 1(1)(a)(one bedroom, shared accommodation)
Stevenage & North Herts	Paragraph 1(1)(a)(one bedroom, shared accommodation)
	Paragraph 1(1)(e)(four bedrooms)
Sussex East	Paragraph 1(1)(a)(one bedroom, shared accommodation)
Swindon	Paragraph 1(1)(a)(one bedroom, shared accommodation)
	Paragraph 1(1)(d)(three bedrooms)
Taff Rhondda	Paragraph 1(1)(a)(one bedroom, shared accommodation)
	Paragraph 1(1)(b)(one bedroom, exclusive use)
	Paragraph 1(1)(e)(four bedrooms)
Teesside	Paragraph 1(1)(b)(one bedroom, exclusive use)
Thanet	Paragraph 1(1)(a)(one bedroom, shared accommodation)
Torfaen	Paragraph 1(1)(e)(four bedrooms)
Walton	Paragraph 1(1)(b)(one bedroom, exclusive use)
	Paragraph 1(1)(c)(two bedrooms)
	Paragraph 1(1)(e)(four bedrooms)
Warwickshire South	Paragraph 1(1)(a)(one bedroom, shared accommodation)
	Paragraph 1(1)(e)(four bedrooms)
West Cheshire	Paragraph 1(1)(a)(one bedroom, shared accommodation)
West Pennine	Paragraph 1(1)(a)(one bedroom, shared accommodation)
	Paragraph 1(1)(b)(one bedroom, exclusive use)
West Wiltshire	Paragraph 1(1)(d)(three bedrooms)
Winchester	Paragraph 1(1)(a)(one bedroom, shared accommodation)
Wolds and Coast	Paragraph 1(1)(a)(one bedroom, shared accommodation)
	Paragraph 1(1)(e)(four bedrooms)
Worcester North	Paragraph 1(1)(d)(three bedrooms)
Worthing	Paragraph 1(1)(e)(four bedrooms)."

SCHEDULE 2
Article 3(3)(b)

Table to be substituted for the table in paragraph 6 of Schedule 3B to the Rent Officers (Housing Benefit Functions) (Scotland) Order 1997

(1) Broad rental market area	*(2) Paragraph of this Schedule defining the category of dwelling*
"Aberdeen and Shire	Paragraph 1(1)(a)(one bedroom, shared accommodation)
	Paragraph 1(1)(b)(one bedroom, exclusive use)
	Paragraph 1(1)(c)(two bedrooms)
	Paragraph 1(1)(d)(three bedrooms)
	Paragraph 1(1)(e)(four bedrooms)
Argyll and Bute	Paragraph 1(1)(a)(one bedroom, shared accommodation)
	Paragraph 1(1)(e)(four bedrooms)
Dundee and Angus	Paragraph 1(1)(e)(four bedrooms)
Fife	Paragraph 1(1)(a)(one bedroom, shared accommodation)
Greater Glasgow	Paragraph 1(1)(e)(four bedrooms)
Lothian	Paragraph 1(1)(c)(two bedrooms)
Renfrewshire/ Inverclyde	Paragraph 1(1)(e)(four bedrooms)
Scottish Borders	Paragraph 1(1)(b)(one bedroom, exclusive use)
South Lanarkshire	Paragraph 1(1)(e)(four bedrooms)
West Dunbartonshire	Paragraph 1(1)(e)(four bedrooms)."

The Marriage and Civil Partnership (Scotland) Act 2014 and Civil Partnership Act 2004 (Consequential Provisions and Modifications) Order 2014

(SI 2014 No.3229)

Made   4th December 2014
Coming into force in accordance with article 1(2)

The Secretary of State makes the following Order in exercise of the powers conferred by sections 104, 112(1) and 113(2) to (5) and (7) of the Scotland Act 1998 and section 259(1) of the Civil Partnership Act 2004.

In accordance with paragraphs 1, 2 and 3 of Schedule 7 to the Scotland Act 1998 and section 259(8) of the Civil Partnership Act 2004, a draft of this Order has been laid before and approved by a resolution of each House of Parliament.

Citation and commencement

1.–(1)   This Order may be cited as the Marriage and Civil Partnership (Scotland) Act 2014 and Civil Partnership Act 2004 (Consequential Provisions and Modifications) Order 2014.

(2)   This Order comes into force on 16th December 2014.

Interpretation

2.   In this Order–
"the 1992 Act" means the Social Security Contributions and Benefits Act 1992;

Extent

3.–(1)   Articles 1 to 3, 7, 29, paragraph 15(7) and paragraph 16 of Schedule 5 extend to England and Wales, Scotland and Northern Ireland.

(2)-(3)   *[Omitted]*

(4)   Articles 4, 5, 8 to 11, and Schedule 1, Schedule 2, Schedule 3, Schedule 4 (except as specified in paragraph (2) of this article), Schedule 5 (except as specified in paragraphs (1), (2) and (3) of this article) and Schedule 6 extend to Scotland only.

(5)   *[Omitted]*

Contrary provision to Schedule 1 and consequential modification of enactments etc. as a result

5.–(1)-(2)   *[Omitted]*

(3)   Schedule 4 (which modifies the Social Security Pensions Act 1975 and the 1992 Act in consequence of the provision made by Schedule 2 to this Order and makes further consequential modifications to those Acts) has effect.

Consequential modifications

29.   Schedules 5 and 6 to this Order (which make consequential modifications to primary and secondary legislation respectively) have effect.

SCHEDULE 4
Article 5(3)
CONSEQUENTIAL MODIFICATION OF THE SOCIAL SECURITY PENSIONS ACT 1975 AND THE SOCIAL SECURITY CONTRIBUTIONS AND BENEFITS ACT 1992

Social Security Contributions and Benefits Act 1992

2.–(1)   The 1992 Act is amended as follows.

(2)-(12)   *[Omitted]*

(13)   In section 137(b) (interpretation of Part 7 and supplementary provisions)–

(a)   in subsection (1), for the definition of "couple" substitute–

''couple'' means–
- (a) two people who are married to, or civil partners of, each other and are members of the same household; or
- (b) two people who are not married to, or civil partners of, each other but are living together as a married couple otherwise than in prescribed circumstances;''; and

(b) omit subsection (1A).
(14)-(20) *[Omitted]*

SCHEDULE 6
Article 29
CONSEQUENTIAL MODIFICATIONS TO SECONDARY LEGISLATION

Housing Benefit and Council Tax Benefit (Decisions and Appeals) Regulations 2001
21. In regulation 1(2) of the Housing Benefit and Council Tax Benefit (Decisions and Appeals) Regulations 2001 (interpretation), for the definition of "couple" substitute–

''couple'' means–
- (a) two people who are married to, or civil partners of, each other and are members of the same household; or
- (b) two people who are not married to, or civil partners of, each other but are living together as a married couple;''.

Housing Benefit Regulations 2006
27. In regulation 2(1) of the Housing Benefit Regulations 2006 (interpretation), for the definition of "couple" substitute–

''couple'' means–
- (a) two people who are married to, or civil partners of, each other and are members of the same household; or
- (b) two people who are not married to, or civil partners of, each other but are living together as a married couple;''.

Housing Benefit (Persons who have attained the qualifying age for state pension credit) Regulations 2006
28. In regulation 2(1) of the Housing Benefit (Persons who have attained the qualifying age for state pension credit) Regulations 2006 (interpretation), for the definition of "couple" substitute–

''couple'' means–
- (a) two people who are married to, or civil partners of, each other and are members of the same household; or
- (b) two people who are not married to, or civil partners of, each other but are living together as a married couple;''.

The Shared Parental Leave and Statutory Shared Parental Pay (Consequential Amendments to Subordinate Legislation) Order 2014

(SI 2014 No.3255)

Made   *9th December 2014*
Laid before Parliament   *10th December 2014*
Coming into force in accordance with article 1(2) and (3)

The Secretary of State makes the following Order in exercise of the powers conferred by section 135(3) and 136(1) and (2) of the Children and Families Act 2014.

Citation and commencement

1.–(1)   This Order may be cited as the Shared Parental Leave and Statutory Shared Parental Pay (Consequential Amendments to Subordinate Legislation) Order 2014.

(2)   The provisions of this Order specified in article 37 come into force on 31st December 2014.

(3)   The remaining provisions of this Order come into force on 5th April 2015.

Housing Benefit Regulations 2006

17.–(1)   The Housing Benefit Regulations 2006 are amended as follows.

(2)   In regulation 2 (interpretation), in the definition of "paternity leave"–

(a)   omit "ordinary";

(b)   omit "or on additional paternity leave by virtue of section 80AA or 80BB of that Act";

(c)   at the appropriate place there is inserted–

"shared parental leave" means leave under section 75E or 75G of the Employment Rights Act 1996;".

(3)   In regulation 6 (remunerative work), in paragraph (7), after "paternity leave" insert ", shared parental leave".

(4)   In regulation 28 (treatment of child care charges)–

(a)   in paragraph (14)(a) after "paternity leave" insert ", shared parental leave";

(b)   in paragraph (14)(a)(i) after "paternity leave" insert ", shared parental leave";

(c)   in paragraph (14)(a)(iii)–

(i)   omit "ordinary";

(ii)   omit "additional statutory paternity pay by virtue of section 171ZEA or 171ZEB of the Act,";

(iii)   after "maternity allowance under section 35 of the Act" insert ", statutory shared parental pay by virtue of section 171ZU or 171ZV of the Act";

(d)   in paragraph (14)(b)(ii)–

(i)   for "ordinary or additional statutory paternity pay or" substitute "statutory paternity pay,"

(ii)   after "statutory adoption pay" insert "or statutory shared parental pay";

(e)   in paragraph (14)(b)(iii)–

(i)   for "ordinary or additional statutory paternity pay or" substitute "statutory paternity pay,";

(ii)   after "statutory adoption pay" insert "or statutory shared parental pay".

(5)   In regulation 35 (earnings of employed earners), in paragraph (1)–

(a)   in sub-paragraph (i)–

(i)   for "ordinary or additional statutory paternity pay or" substitute "statutory paternity pay,";

(ii)   after "statutory adoption pay," insert "statutory shared parental pay";

(b)   in sub-paragraph (j) after "adoption leave" insert "or shared parental leave".

(6)   In regulation 36 (calculation of net earnings of employed earners), in paragraph (3)(d)–
    (a)   for "ordinary or additional statutory paternity pay or" substitute "statutory paternity pay,";
    (b)   after "statutory adoption pay" insert "or statutory shared parental pay".
(7)   In regulation 75E (exception to the benefit cap: current or recent work), in paragraph (4) for "or adoption leave" substitute ", adoption leave or shared parental leave".

Housing Benefit (Persons who have attained the qualifying age for state pension credit) Regulations 2006

18.–(1)   The Housing Benefit (Persons who have attained the qualifying age for state pension credit) 2006 is amended as follows.
(2)   In regulation 2 (interpretation)–
    (a)   in the definition of "paternity leave''–
        (i)   omit "ordinary";
        (ii)   omit "or on additional paternity leave by virtue of section 80AA or 80BB of that Act";
    (b)   at the appropriate place there is inserted–

''shared parental leave" means leave under section 75E or 75G of the Employment Rights Act 1996;".

(3)   In regulation 6 (remunerative work), in paragraph (7) for "or adoption leave" substitute ", adoption leave or shared parental leave".
(4)   In regulation 29 (meaning of "income"), in paragraph (1)(j)–
    (a)   in sub-paragraph (xvi) omit "ordinary";
    (b)   omit sub-paragraph (xvia);
    (c)   after sub-paragraph (xvii) insert–

"(xviia) statutory shared parental pay payable under Part 12ZC of the Act;".

(5)   In regulation 31 (treatment of child care charges)–
    (a)   in paragraph (14) for "or adoption leave" substitute ", adoption leave or shared parental leave";
    (b)   in paragraph (14)(a) for "or adoption leave" substitute ", adoption leave or shared parental leave";
    (c)   in paragraph (14)(c)–
        (i)   omit "ordinary";
        (ii)   omit "additional statutory paternity pay by virtue of section 171ZEA or 171ZEB of the Act,"
        (iii) after "section 171ZL of the Act" insert ", statutory shared parental pay by virtue of section 171ZU or 171ZV of the Act";
    (d)   in paragraph (15)(b)–
        (i)   omit "ordinary or additional";
        (ii)   for "or statutory adoption pay" substitute ", statutory adoption pay or statutory shared parental pay";
    (e)   in paragraph 15(c)–
        (i)   omit "ordinary or additional";
        (ii)   for "or statutory adoption pay" substitute ", statutory adoption pay or statutory shared parental pay";
(6)   In regulation 35 (earnings of employed earners), in paragraph (1)–
    (a)   in paragraph (i) omit "ordinary";
    (b)   omit paragraph (ia);
    (c)   after paragraph (j) insert–

"(ja) statutory shared parental pay payable under Part 12ZC of the Act;".

(7)   In regulation 36 (calculation of net earnings of employed earners), in paragraph (2)(d)–
(a)   omit "ordinary or additional";
(b)   for "or statutory adoption pay" substitute ", statutory adoption pay or statutory shared parental pay".

Council Tax Reduction (Scotland) Regulations 2012
23.–(1)   The Council Tax Reduction (Scotland) Regulations 2012 are amended as follows.
(2)   In regulation 2 (interpretation), in paragraph (1)–
(a)   omit the definition of "additional statutory paternity pay";
(b)   omit the definition of "ordinary statutory paternity pay";
(c)   in the definition of "paternity leave"–
    (i)   omit "ordinary";
    (ii)   omit "or on additional paternity leave by virtue of section 80AA or 80BB of that Act";
(d)   at the appropriate places there is inserted–

"shared parental leave" means leave by virtue of section 75E or 75G of the Employment Rights Act 1996;"; and
"statutory shared parental pay" means statutory shared parental pay under section 171ZU or 171ZV of the 1992 Act;".

(3)   In regulation 6 (remunerative work), in paragraph (7) after "paternity leave" insert ", shared parental leave".
(4)   In regulation 28 (treatment of child care charges)–
(a)   in paragraph (15)–
    (i)   after "paternity leave" in both places where those words appear insert ", shared parental leave";
    (ii)   for "ordinary statutory paternity pay" substitute "statutory paternity pay";
    (iii)   omit ", additional statutory paternity pay by virtue of section 171ZEA or 171ZEB of the 1992 Act";
    (iv)   for "statutory adoption pay" substitute "statutory shared parental pay, statutory adoption pay";
(b)   in paragraph (16)–
    (i)   after "paternity leave" insert ", shared parental leave";
    (ii)   omit "ordinary or additional" in both places where those words appear;
    (iii)   for "or statutory adoption pay ends" in both places where those words appear substitute ", statutory shared parental pay or statutory adoption pay ends".
(5)   In regulation 34 (earnings of employed earners)–
(a)   in paragraph (1)(j)–
    (i)   omit "ordinary or additional";
    (ii)   for "or statutory adoption pay" substitute ", statutory shared parental pay or statutory adoption pay";
(b)   in paragraph (1)(k), after "paternity leave" insert ", shared parental leave".
(6)   In regulation 35 (calculation of net earnings of employed earners), in paragraph (3)(d)–
(a)   omit "ordinary or additional";
(b)   for "or statutory adoption pay" substitute ", statutory shared parental pay or statutory adoption pay".

Council Tax Reduction (State Pension Credit) (Scotland) Regulations 2012
24.–(1)   The Council Tax Reduction (State Pension Credit) (Scotland) Regulations 2012 are amended as follows.
(2)   In regulation 2 (interpretation), in paragraph (1)–
(a)   omit the definition of "additional statutory paternity pay";

    (b)   omit the definition of "ordinary statutory paternity pay";
    (c)   in the definition of "paternity leave"–
          (i)   omit "ordinary";
          (ii)   omit "or on additional paternity leave by virtue of sections 80AA or 80BB of that Act";
    (d)   at the appropriate places there is inserted–
          (i)   "shared parental leave" means leave under section 75E or 75G of the Employment Rights Act 1996;";
          (ii)   "statutory paternity pay" means statutory paternity pay under section 171ZA or 171ZB of the 1992 Act;";
          (iii)   "statutory shared parental pay" means statutory shared parental pay under section 171ZU or 171ZV of the 1992 Act;".

    (3)   In regulation 6 (remunerative work), in paragraph (7), after "paternity leave" insert ", shared parental leave".

    (4)   In regulation 27 (meaning of "income"), in paragraph (1)(j)–
    (a)   in sub-paragraph (xviii) for "ordinary statutory paternity pay or additional statutory paternity pay" substitute "statutory paternity pay";
    (b)   after sub-paragraph (xviii) insert–

"(xviiia) statutory shared parental pay;".

    (5)   In regulation 29 (treatment of child care charges)–
    (a)   in paragraph (15)–
          (i)   after "paternity leave" in both places where those words appear insert ", shared parental leave";
          (ii)   for "ordinary statutory paternity pay" substitute "statutory paternity pay";
          (iii)   omit ", additional statutory paternity pay";
          (iv)   for "statutory adoption pay" substitute "statutory shared parental pay, statutory adoption pay";
    (b)   in paragraph (16)–
          (i)   after "paternity leave" insert ", shared parental leave";
          (ii)   for "ordinary statutory paternity pay" in both places where those words appear substitute "statutory paternity pay";
          (iii)   omit ", additional statutory paternity pay" in both places where those words appear;
          (iv)   for "or statutory adoption pay ends" in both places where those words appear, substitute ", statutory shared parental pay or statutory adoption pay ends".

    (6)   In regulation 32 (earnings of employed earners), in paragraph (1)–
    (a)   in sub-paragraph (i) for "ordinary statutory paternity pay or additional statutory paternity pay" substitute "statutory paternity pay";
    (b)   after sub-paragraph (i) insert–

"(ia) statutory shared parental pay;".

    (7)   In regulation 33 (calculation of net earnings of employed earners), in paragraph (2)(d)–
    (a)   for "ordinary statutory paternity pay" substitute "statutory paternity pay";
    (b)   omit ", additional statutory paternity pay";
    (c)   for "or statutory adoption pay" substitute ", statutory shared parental pay or statutory adoption pay".

Council Tax Reduction Schemes (Prescribed Requirements) (England) Regulations 2012

    27.–(1)   The Council Tax Reduction Schemes (Prescribed Requirements) (England) Regulations 2012 is amended as follows.
    (2)   In regulation 2 (interpretation), in paragraph (1)–

(a)   in the definition of "paternity leave"–
      (i)   omit "ordinary";
      (ii)   omit "or on additional paternity leave by virtue of section 80AA or 80BB of that Act";
(b)   at the appropriate place there is inserted–

"shared parental leave" means leave under section 75E or 75G of the Employment Rights Act 1996;".

(3)   In regulation 10 (remunerative work), in paragraph (7), after "paternity leave" insert ", shared parental leave".

(4)   In Schedule 1 (pensioners), in Part 6 (income and capital)–

(a)   in paragraph 16 (meaning of "income")–
      (i)   in sub-paragraph (1)(j)(xvi) omit "ordinary";
      (ii)   omit sub-paragraph (1)(j)(xvii);
      (iii) after subparagraph (1)(j)(xvi) insert–

"(xvia) statutory shared parental pay under Part 12ZC of that Act;";

(b)   in paragraph 18 (earnings of employed earners)–
      (i)   in sub-paragraph (1)(j) omit "ordinary";
      (ii)   omit sub-paragraph (1)(k);
      (iii) after sub-paragraph (1)(j) insert–

"(ja)   statutory shared parental pay under Part 12ZC of that Act;";

(c)   in paragraph 19 (calculation of net earnings of employed earners), in sub-paragraph (2)(d) for "ordinary or additional statutory paternity pay" substitute "statutory paternity pay, statutory shared parental pay";
(d)   in paragraph 25 (treatment of child care charges), in sub-paragraph (14)–
      (i)   after "paternity leave" in both places where those words occur insert ", shared parental leave";
      (ii)   omit "ordinary";
      (iii) omit "additional statutory paternity pay by virtue of section 171ZEA or 171ZEB of that Act";
      (iv) after "under section 35 of that Act" insert ", statutory shared parental pay by virtue of section 171ZU or 171ZV of that Act";
(e)   in paragraph 25, in sub-paragraph (15)–
      (i)   after "paternity leave" insert ", shared parental leave";
      (ii)   for "or statutory adoption pay ends" in both places where those words occur substitute "statutory shared paternity pay or statutory adoption pay ends".

Transitional provisions

35.–(1)   The amendments made by this Order in those articles which come into force on 5ᵗʰ April 2015 in accordance with 1(3) (amendments relating to references to ordinary and additional paternity leave and to ordinary and additional statutory paternity pay) do not have effect in relation to–
(a)   ordinary statutory paternity pay which is paid;
(b)   additional statutory paternity pay which is paid;
(c)   a period in respect of which additional statutory paternity pay is payable which begins, or continues;
(d)   ordinary paternity leave which is taken; or
(e)   additional paternity leave which is taken;
on or after 5th April 2015.

(2)   In this article–

"additional paternity leave" means leave under section 80AA or 80BB of the Employment Rights Act 1996(a);

"additional statutory paternity pay" means pay under section 171ZEA or 171ZEB of the Social Security Contributions and Benefits Act 1992;

"ordinary paternity leave" means leave under section 80A or 80B of the Employment Rights Act 1996;

"ordinary statutory paternity pay" means pay under section 171ZA or 171ZB of the Social Security Contributions and Benefits Act 1992.

Provisions coming into force on 31st December 2014

37.   The provisions specified in article 1(2) are–

(a)   this article;

(b)-(n) *[Omitted]*

(o)   article 17(1), (2)(c), (3), (4)(a), (b), (c)(iii), (d)(ii) and (e)(ii), (5)(a)(ii) and (b), (6)(b) and (7);

(p)   article 18(1), (2)(b), (3), (4)(c), (5)(a), (b), (c)(iii), (d)(ii) and (e)(ii), (6)(c) and (7)(b);

(q)-(t) *[Omitted]*

(u)   article 23(1), (2)(d), (3), (4)(a)(i) and (iv) and (b)(i) and (iii), (5)(b) and (c) and (6)(b);

(v)   article 24(1), (2)(d)(i) and (iii), (3), (4)(b), (5)(a)(i) and (iv) and (b)(i) and (iv), (6)(b) and (7)(c);

(w)-(x) *[Omitted]*

(y)   article 27(1), (2)(b), (3), (4)(a)(iii), (b)(iii), (c), (d)(i) and (iv) and (e);

(z)-(ff) *[Omitted]*

(gg)   article 35;

(hh)   *[Omitted]*.

The Council Tax Reduction Schemes (Prescribed Requirements) (England) (Amendment) (No.2) Regulations 2014

(SI 2014 No.3312)

Made   *16th December 2014*
Laid before Parliament   *18th December 2014*
Coming into force   *12th January 2015*

The Secretary of State makes the following Regulations in exercise of the powers conferred by section 113(1) and (2) of, and paragraph 2 of Schedule 1A to, the Local Government Finance Act 1992:

Citation, commencement and application
1.–(1) These Regulations may be cited as the Council Tax Reduction Schemes (Prescribed Requirements) (England) (Amendment) (No. 2) Regulations 2014 and come into force on 12th January 2015.

(2) These Regulations apply in relation to council tax reduction schemes made by billing authorities for financial years beginning on or after 1st April 2015.

Amendment of the Council Tax Reduction Schemes (Prescribed Requirements) (England) Regulations 2012
2.–(1) The Council Tax Reduction Schemes (Prescribed Requirements) (England) Regulations 2012 are amended as follows.

(2) In regulation 2 (interpretation)–

(a) in paragraph (1)–

(i) for the definition of "contributory employment and support allowance" substitute–

"contributory employment and support allowance" means an allowance under Part 1 of the Welfare Reform Act 2007 as amended by the provisions of Schedule 3, and Part 1 of Schedule 14, to the Welfare Reform Act 2012 that remove references to an income-related allowance and a contributory allowance under Part 1 of the Welfare Reform Act 2007 as that Part has effect apart from those provisions;";

(ii) omit the definition of "service user group";

(b) after paragraph (7) insert–

"(8) References in these Regulations to an applicant participating as a service user are to–

(a) a person who is being consulted by or on behalf of–

(i) a body which has a statutory duty to provide services in the field of health, social care or social housing; or

(ii) a body which conducts research or undertakes monitoring for the purpose of planning or improving such services, in their capacity as a user, potential user, carer of a user or person otherwise affected by the provision of those services; or

(b) the carer of a person consulted as described in sub-paragraph (a) where the carer is not being consulted as described in that sub-paragraph.".

(3) In regulation 6 (meaning of "family")–

(a) omit the "or" following paragraph (3)(a);

(b) after paragraph (3)(b) insert–

"; or
(c) entitled to an award of universal credit.".

(4) In regulation 12(5) (persons treated as not being in Great Britain)–

(a)   in sub-paragraph (h) omit ", an income-based jobseeker's allowance";
(b)   omit the "or" following sub-paragraph (h);
(c)   after sub-paragraph (h) add–

"(ha) in receipt of an income-based jobseeker's allowance and has a right to reside other than a right to reside falling within paragraph (4); or".

(5)   In Schedule 1 (pensioners: matters that must be included in an authority's scheme)–
(a)   in paragraph 8 (non-dependant deductions)–
    (i)   in sub-paragraph (1)(a) for "£11.25" substitute "£11.36";
    (ii)   in sub-paragraph (1)(b) for "£3.70" substitute "£3.74";
    (iii)   in sub-paragraph (2)(a) for "£188.00" substitute "£189.00";
    (iv)   in sub-paragraph (2)(b) for "£188.00", "£326.00" and "£7.45" substitute "£189.00", "£328.00" and "£7.52" respectively;
    (v)   in sub-paragraph (2)(c) for "£326.00", "£406.00" and "£9.40" substitute "£328.00", "£408.00" and "£9.49" respectively;
    (vi)   in sub-paragraph (8)–
        (aa)   omit the "or" following paragraph (a);
        (bb)   after paragraph (b) add–

"; or
(c)   who is entitled to an award of universal credit where the award is calculated on the basis that the person does not have any earned income.";

    (vii)   after sub-paragraph (11) insert–

"(11A)   For the purposes of sub-paragraph (8), "earned income" has the meaning given in regulation 52 of the Universal Credit Regulations 2013.";

(b)   in the following provisions for "applicant's participation in a service user group" substitute "applicant participating as a service user"–
    (i)   paragraph 18(2)(f) (earnings of employed earners);
    (ii)   paragraph 22(12) (notional income);
    (iii)   paragraph 23(3) (income paid to third parties);
(c)   in paragraph 25 (treatment of child care charges)–
    (i)   in sub-paragraph (10)(c) and (e) after "Employment and Support Allowance Regulations 2008" insert "or the Employment and Support Allowance Regulations 2013";
    (ii)   in sub-paragraph (10)(g) for "or allowance to which sub-paragraph (vii) or (viii)" substitute "or allowance or payment to which sub-paragraph (v), (vii) or (viii)";
    (iii)   in sub-paragraph (13)(b) for "would be payable but for" substitute "has ceased to be payable by virtue of";
(d)   in the following provisions for "social security contributions" substitute "national insurance contributions"–
    (i)   paragraph 28(c) (disregard of changes in tax, contributions etc);
    (ii)   in paragraph 29 (calculation of net profit of self-employed earners)–
        (aa)   sub-paragraph (1)(b)(i);
        (bb)   sub-paragraph (2)(b)(ii);
        (cc)   sub-paragraph (8)(a)(ii);
    (iii)   paragraph 30(3) (calculation of tax and contributions of self-employed earners).
(6)   In Schedule 2 (applicable amounts)–
(a)   in column (2) of the Table in paragraph 1–
    (i)   in sub-paragraph (1)(a) for "£148.35" substitute "£151.20";
    (ii)   in sub-paragraph (1)(b) for "£165.15" substitute "£166.05";

      (iii)   in sub-paragraph (2)(a) for "£226.50" substitute "£230.85";
      (iv)   in sub-paragraph (2)(b) for "£247.20" substitute "£248.28";
      (v)   in sub-paragraph (3)(a) for "£226.50" substitute "£230.85";
      (vi)   in sub-paragraph (3)(b) for "£78.15" substitute "£79.65";
      (vii)   in sub-paragraph (4)(a) for "£247.20" substitute "£248.28";
      (viii)   in sub-paragraph (4)(b) for "£82.05" substitute "£82.26";
(b)   in column (2) of the Table in paragraph 2 for "£66.33" in each place where it occurs substitute "£66.90";
(c)   in the second column of the Table in Part 4–
      (i)   in paragraph (1)(a) and (b)(i) for "£61.10" substitute "£61.85";
      (ii)   in paragraph (1)(b)(ii) for "£122.20" substitute "£123.70";
      (iii)   in paragraph (2) for "£24.08" substitute "£24.43";
      (iv)   in paragraph (3) for "£59.50" substitute "£60.06";
      (v)   in paragraph (4) for "£34.20" substitute "£34.60".
(7)   In column (1) of the Table in paragraph 1 of Schedule 3 (amount of alternative maximum council tax reduction)–
(a)   in paragraph (b)(i) for "£185.00" substitute "£187.00";
(b)   in paragraph (b)(ii) for "£185.00" and "£241.00" substitute "£187.00" and "£243.00" respectively.
(8)   In Schedule 4 (sums disregarded from applicant's earnings)–
(a)   in paragraph 5(1)(d)(ii) after "Employment and Support Allowance Regulations 2008" insert "or regulation 7 of the Employment and Support Allowance Regulations 2013";
(b)   in paragraph 6(6)(a) after "Employment and Support Allowance Regulations 2008" insert "or regulation 39(1)(a), (b) or (c) of the Employment and Support Allowance Regulations 2013".
(9)   In paragraph 19(2)(b) of Schedule 5 (amounts to be disregarded in the calculation of income other than earnings) for "£57.35" substitute "£57.90".
(10)   In Schedule 6 (capital disregards)–
(a)   in paragraph 21(2)–
      (i)   omit the "or" following paragraph (o);
      (ii)   after paragraph (p) insert–

"; or
(q)   universal credit.";

(b)   in paragraph 22(2)(b) after "Jobseeker's Allowance Regulations" insert "1996";
(c)   in paragraph 22(2)(e) after "Employment and Support Allowance Regulations" insert "2008".

Transitional provision

3.–(1)   The amendment in regulation 2(4) does not apply to a person who, on 31st March 2015–
(a)   is liable to pay council tax at a reduced rate by virtue of a council tax reduction under an authority's scheme established under section 13A(2) of the Act; and
(b)   is entitled to an income-based jobseeker's allowance,
until the first of the events in paragraph (2) occurs.
(2)   The events are–
(a)   the person makes a new application for a reduction under an authority's scheme established under section 13A(2) of the Act; or
(b)   the person ceases to be entitled to an income-based jobseeker's allowance.
(3)   In this regulation "the Act" means the Local Government Finance Act 1992.

The Housing Benefit and Housing Benefit (Persons who have attained the qualifying age for state pension credit) (Income from earnings) (Amendment) Regulations 2015

(SI 2015 No.6)

Made	*6th January 2015*
Laid before Parliament	*12th January 2015*
Coming into force	*9th February 2015*

The Secretary of State for Work and Pensions makes the following Regulations in exercise of the powers conferred by sections 136(3) and (4), 136A(3) and 137(1) of the Social Security, Contributions and Benefits Act 1992.

The Social Security Advisory Committee has agreed the proposals in respect of these Regulations should not be referred to it.

In accordance with section 176(1) of the Social Security Administration Act 1992, consultation has taken place with organisations which appear to the Secretary of State to be representative of the authorities concerned.

Citation and commencement
1.   These Regulations may be cited as the Housing Benefit and Housing Benefit (Persons who have attained the qualifying age for state pension credit) (Income from earnings) (Amendment) Regulations 2015 and come into force on 9th February 2015.

Amendment to the Housing Benefit Regulations 2006
2.–(1)   The Housing Benefit Regulations 2006 are amended as follows.

(2)   In paragraph (2) of regulation 29 (Average weekly earnings of employed earners) after "if he has received any earnings" insert "or expects to receive an amount of earnings".

(3)   After regulation 29 (Average weekly earnings of employed earners) insert–

"Date on which income consisting of earnings from employment as an employed earner are taken into account

29A.–(1)   A claimant's average weekly earnings from employment estimated pursuant to regulation 29 (Average weekly earnings of employed earners) and Section 3 (Employed earners) of this Part shall be taken into account–

   (a)   in the case of a claim, on the date that the claim was made or treated as made and the first day of each benefit week thereafter, regardless of whether those earnings were actually received in that benefit week;

   (b)   in the case of a claim or award where the claimant commences employment, the first day of the benefit week following the date the claimant commences that employment, and the first day of each benefit week thereafter, regardless of whether those earnings were actually received in that benefit week; or

   (c)   in the case of a claim or award where the claimant's average weekly earnings from employment change, the first day of the benefit week following the date of the change, and the beginning of each benefit week thereafter, regardless of whether those earnings were actually received in that benefit week.".

Amendments to the Housing Benefit (Persons who have attained the qualifying age for state pension credit) Regulations 2006
3.–(1)   Regulation 33 (Calculation of weekly income) of the Housing Benefit (Persons who have attained the qualifying age for state pension credit) Regulations 2006 is amended as follows.

(2)   In paragraph (1) after "paragraph (2)" insert ", (2A), (3A)".

(3)   After paragraph (2) insert–

"(2A)   Income calculated pursuant to paragraph (2) shall be taken into account–

    (a)   in the case of a claim, on the date the claim was made or treated as made, and the first day of each benefit week thereafter;

    (b)   in the case of a claim or award where the claimant commences employment, the first day of the benefit week following the date the claimant commences that employment, and the first day of each benefit week thereafter; or

    (c)   in the case of a claim or award where the claimant's average weekly earnings from employment change, the first day of the benefit week following the date the claimant's earnings from employment change so as to require recalculation under this paragraph, and the first day of each benefit week thereafter,

regardless of whether those earnings were actually received in that benefit week.".

(4)   After paragraph (3) insert–

"(3A)   A claimant's earnings from employment as an employed earner not calculated pursuant to paragraph (2) shall be taken into account–

    (a)   in the case of a claim, on the date that the claim was made or treated as made and the first day of each benefit week thereafter;

    (b)   in the case of a claim or award where the claimant commences employment, the first day of the benefit week following the date the claimant commences that employment, and the first day of each benefit week thereafter; or

    (c)   in the case of a claim or award where the claimant's average weekly earnings from employment change, the first day of the benefit week following the date of the change, and the beginning of each benefit week thereafter,

regardless of whether those earnings were actually received in that benefit week.".

The Welfare Reform Act 2012 (Commencement No.21 and Transitional and Transitory Provisions) Order 2015

(SI 2015 No.33)

Made	*19th January 2015*

The Secretary of State for Work and Pensions makes the following Order in exercise of the powers conferred by section 150(3) and (4)(a), (b)(i) and (c) of the Welfare Reform Act 2012:

Citation
1.   This Order may be cited as the Welfare Reform Act 2012 (Commencement No. 21 and Transitional and Transitory Provisions) Order 2015.

Interpretation
2.–(1)   In this Order–
"the No. 9 Order" means the Welfare Reform Act 2012 (Commencement No. 9 and Transitional and Transitory Provisions and Commencement No. 8 and Savings and Transitional Provisions (Amendment)) Order 2013;

Transitional provision: claims for housing benefit, income support or a tax credit
6.–(1)   Except as provided by paragraphs (2) to (5), a person may not make a claim for housing benefit, income support or a tax credit (in the latter case, whether or not as part of a Tax Credits Act couple) on any date where, if that person made a claim for universal credit on that date (in the capacity, whether as a single person or as part of a couple, in which he or she is permitted to claim universal credit under the Universal Credit Regulations 2013), the provisions of the Act listed in Schedule 2 to the No. 9 Order would come into force under article 3(1) and (2)(a) of this Order in relation to that claim for universal credit.

(2)   Paragraph (1) does not apply to a claim for housing benefit in respect of specified accommodation.

(3)   Paragraph (1) does not apply to a claim for housing benefit or a tax credit where–

(a)   in the case of a claim for housing benefit, the claim is made by a person who has reached the qualifying age for state pension credit, or by a person who is a member of a State Pension Credit Act couple the other member of which has reached that age;

(b)   *[Omitted]*

(4)-(6)   *[Omitted]*

(7)   Subject to paragraph (8), for the purposes of this article–

(a)   a claim for housing benefit, income support or a tax credit is made by a person on the date on which he or she takes any action which results in a decision on a claim being required under the relevant Regulations; and

(b)   it is irrelevant that the effect of any provision of the relevant Regulations is that, for the purpose of those Regulations, the claim is made or treated as made on a date that is earlier than the date on which that action is taken.

(8)   Where under the provisions referred to in paragraph (9), a claim for housing benefit or income support is treated as made at a date that is earlier than the date on which the action referred to in paragraph (7)(a) is taken, the claim is treated as made on that earlier date.

(9)   The provisions referred to are–

(a)   in the case of a claim for housing benefit, regulation 83(4E), (4F), (5)(d) or (8) of the Housing Benefit Regulations 2006 ("the 2006 Regulations") or, as the case may be, regulation 64(5F), (5G), (6)(d) or (9) of the Housing Benefit (Persons who have attained the qualifying age for state pension credit) Regulations 2006 ("the 2006 (SPC) Regulations")); or

(b)   *[Omitted]*

(10)   For the purposes of this article–

(a)   "couple" (apart from in the expressions "State Pension Credit Act couple" and "Tax Credit Act couple"), has the meaning given in section 39 of the Act;

(b)   "housing benefit" means housing benefit under section 130 of the Social Security Contributions and Benefits Act 1992;

(c)   *[Omitted]*

(d)   "qualifying age for state pension credit" means the qualifying age referred to in section 1(6) of the State Pension Credit Act 2002;

(e)   the "relevant Regulations" means–

    (i)   in the case of a claim for housing benefit, the 2006 Regulations or, as the case may be, the 2006 (SPC) Regulations;

    (ii)-(iii) *[Omitted]*

(f)   "specified accommodation" means accommodation to which one or more of subparagraphs (2) to (5) of paragraph 3A of Schedule 1 to the Universal Credit Regulations 2013 applies;

(g)   "state pension credit" means state pension credit under the State Pension Credit Act 2002;

(h)   "State Pension Credit Act couple" means a couple as defined in section 17 of the State Pension Credit Act 2002;

(i)-(j) *[Omitted]*

The Council Tax Reduction Schemes (Prescribed Requirements and Default Scheme) (Wales) (Amendment) Regulations 2015
(SI 2015 No.44)(W.3)

Made   *20th January 2015*
Coming into force in accordance with regulation 1(2)

The Welsh Ministers make the following Regulations in exercise of the powers conferred upon them by section 13A(4) and (5) of, and paragraphs 2 to 7 of Schedule 1B to, the Local Government Finance Act 1992.

In accordance with section 13A(8) of that Act, a draft of this instrument has been laid before and approved by resolution of the National Assembly for Wales.

Title, commencement and interpretation
1.–(1) The title of these Regulations is the Council Tax Reduction Schemes (Prescribed Requirements and Default Scheme) (Wales) (Amendment) Regulations 2015.

(2) These Regulations come into force the day after the day on which they are made.

(3) These Regulations apply in relation to a council tax reduction scheme made for a financial year beginning on or after 1 April 2015.

(4) In these Regulations "council tax reduction scheme" ("cynllun gostyngiadau'r dreth gyngor") means a scheme made by a billing authority in accordance with the Council Tax Reduction Schemes and Prescribed Requirements (Wales) Regulations 2013, or the scheme that applies in default by virtue of paragraph 6(1)(e) of Schedule 1B to the Local Government Finance Act 1992.

Amendments to the Council Tax Reduction Schemes and Prescribed Requirements (Wales) Regulations 2013
2. The Council Tax Reduction Schemes and Prescribed Requirements (Wales) Regulations 2013 are amended in accordance with regulations 3 to 13.

3. In regulation 2(1) (interpretation)–

(a) for the definition of "contributory employment and support allowance", substitute–

"contributory employment and support allowance" ("lwfans cyflogaeth a chymorth cyfrannol") means an allowance under Part 1 of the Welfare Reform Act 2007 as amended by the provisions of Schedule 3, and Part 1 of Schedule 14, to the Welfare Reform Act 2012 that remove references to an income-related allowance, and a contributory allowance under Part 1 of the Welfare Reform Act 2007 as that Part has effect apart from those provisions;";

(b) at the appropriate place insert–

"shared parental leave" ("absenoldeb rhiant a rennir") means leave by virtue of regulations made under section 75E or 75G of the Employment Rights Act 1996;".

4. In regulation 10 (remunerative work), in paragraph (7) after "paternity leave" insert "', shared parental leave".

5. In regulation 18 (revisions to and replacement of schemes)–

(a) in paragraph (4) for "Regulation 17" substitute "Subject to paragraph (6), regulation 17";

(b) after paragraph (5) insert–

"(6) Regulation 17(1) does not apply where a scheme is revised in consequence only of one or more amendments made to these Regulations."

6.   In regulation 28(5) (persons treated as not being in Great Britain)–

(a)   in sub-paragraph (j) omit '', an income-based jobseeker's allowance'';

(b)   after sub-paragraph (k)–

    (i)   omit ''.'';

    (ii)   add–

''; or

(l)   in receipt of an income-based jobseeker's allowance and has a right to reside other than a right to reside falling within paragraph (4)(a) to (d).''

7.   In Schedule 1 (determining eligibility for a reduction: pensioners)–

(a)   in paragraph 3 (non-dependant deductions: pensioners)–

    (i)   in sub-paragraph (1)(a) for ''£11.30'' substitute ''£11.75'';

    (ii)   in sub-paragraph (1)(b) for ''£3.75'' substitute ''£3.90'';

    (iii)   in sub-paragraph (2)(a) for ''£188.00'' substitute ''£189.00'';

    (iv)   in sub-paragraph (2)(b) for ''£188.00'', ''£326.00'' and ''£7.50'' substitute ''£189.00'', ''£328.00'' and ''£7.80'' respectively;

    (v)   in sub-paragraph (2)(c) for ''£326.00'', ''£406.00'' and ''£9.45'' substitute ''£328.00'', ''£408.00'' and ''£9.85'' respectively;

    (vi)   in sub-paragraph (8)–

        (aa)   omit the "or" following paragraph (a);

        (bb)   after paragraph (b) add–

''; or

(c)   who is entitled to an award of universal credit where the award is calculated on the basis that the person does not have any earned income.'';

    (vii)   after sub-paragraph (9) insert–

''(10)   For the purposes of sub-paragraph (8), "earned income" ("incwm a enillir") has the meaning given in regulation 52 of the Universal Credit Regulations 2013.'';

(b)   in paragraph 10(1) (meaning of "income": pensioners)–

    (i)   in paragraph (j)(xvi) omit "ordinary";

    (ii)   after paragraph (j)(xvi) insert–

''(xvia) statutory shared parental pay payable under Part 12ZC of the SSCBA;'';

(c)   in paragraph 12 (earnings of employed earners: pensioners), after sub-paragraph (1)(j) insert–

''(ja)   statutory shared parental pay payable under Part 12ZC of the SSCBA;'';

(d)   in paragraph 13 (calculation of net earnings of employed earners: pensioners), in subparagraph (2)(d)–

    (i)   omit "ordinary or additional";

    (ii)   after "statutory paternity pay" insert '', statutory shared parental pay'';

(e)   in paragraph 19 (treatment of child care charges: pensioners)–

    (i)   in sub-paragraph (11)(c) and (e) after "Employment and Support Allowance Regulations 2008" insert "or the Employment and Support Allowance Regulations 2013";

    (ii)   in sub-paragraph (15)–

        (aa)   after "paternity leave" in both places where those words occur, insert '', shared parental leave'';

        (bb)   omit "ordinary";

        (cc)   after "maternity allowance under section 35 of that Act" insert '', statutory shared parental pay by virtue of section 171ZU or 171ZV of that Act'';

        (iii)   in sub-paragraph (16)–
          (aa)   after "paternity leave" insert ", shared parental leave";
          (bb)   omit "ordinary or additional" in both places where those words occur;
          (cc)   after "statutory paternity pay" in both places where those words occur, insert ", statutory shared parental pay".

8.   In Schedule 2 (applicable amounts: pensioners)–

(a)   in column (2) of the Table in paragraph 1 (personal allowances)–
    (i)   in sub-paragraph (1) for "£148.35" and "£165.15" substitute "£151.20" and "£166.05" respectively;
    (ii)   in sub-paragraph (2) for "£226.50" and "£247.20" substitute "£230.85" and "£248.30" respectively;
    (iii) in sub-paragraph (3) for "£226.50" and "£78.15" substitute "£230.85" and "£79.65" respectively;
    (iv) in sub-paragraph (4) for "£247.20" and "£82.05" substitute "£248.30" and "£82.25" respectively;

(b)   in column (2) of the Table in paragraph 2 (child or young person amounts), for "£66.33" in each place where it occurs substitute "£66.90";

(c)   in paragraph 3 (family premium) for "£17.40" substitute "£17.45";

(d)   in the second column of the Table in Part 4 (amounts of premium specified in Part 3)–
    (i)   in sub-paragraph (1) for "£61.10" in each place where it occurs substitute "£61.85" and for "£122.20" substitute "£123.70";
    (ii)   in sub-paragraph (2) for "£24.08" substitute "£24.43";
    (iii) in sub-paragraph (3) for "£59.50" substitute "£60.06";
    (iv) in sub-paragraph (4) for "£34.20" substitute "£34.60";

9.   In Schedule 3 (sums disregarded from applicant's earnings: pensioners)–

(a)   in paragraph 5(1)(d)(ii) after "Employment and Support Allowance Regulations 2008" insert "or regulation 7 of the Employment and Support Allowance Regulations 2013";

(b)   in paragraph 6(6)(a), after "Employment and Support Allowance Regulations 2008" insert "or regulation 39(1)(a), (b) or (c) of the Employment and Support Allowance Regulations 2013".

10.   In Schedule 6 (determining eligibility for a reduction)–

(a)   in paragraph 5 (non-dependant deductions: persons who are not pensioners)–
    (i)   in sub-paragraph (1)(a) for "£11.30" substitute "£11.75";
    (ii)   in sub-paragraph (1)(b) for "£3.75" substitute "£3.90";
    (iii) in sub-paragraph (2)(a) for "£188.00" substitute "£189.00";
    (iv) in sub-paragraph (2)(b) for "£188.00", "£326.00" and "£7.50" substitute "£189.00", "£328.00" and "£7.80" respectively;
    (v)   in sub-paragraph (2)(c) for "£326.00", "£406.00" and "£9.45" substitute "£328.00", "£408.00" and "£9.85" respectively;
    (vi) in sub-paragraph (8)–
      (aa) omit the "or" following paragraph (a);
      (bb) after paragraph (b) insert–

"; or
(c)   who is entitled to an award of universal credit where the award is calculated on the basis that the person does not have any earned income.";

    (vii) after sub-paragraph (9) insert–

"(10) For the purposes of sub-paragraph (8), "earned income" ("incwm a enillir") has the meaning given in regulation 52 of the Universal Credit Regulations 2013.";

(b)   in paragraph 14 (earnings of employed earners: persons who are not pensioners)–
    (i)   in sub-paragraph (1)(j) after "statutory paternity pay" insert ", statutory shared parental pay";

(ii)　in sub-paragraph (1)(k) after "paternity leave" insert ", shared parental leave";

(c)　in paragraph 15 (calculation of net earnings of employed earners: persons who are not pensioners), in sub-paragraph (3)(d)–

(i)　omit "ordinary or additional";

(ii)　after "statutory paternity pay" insert ", statutory shared parental pay";

(d)　in paragraph 17 (calculation of income other than earnings: persons who are not pensioners) in sub-paragraph (4), after "Employment and Support Allowance Regulations 2008" insert "or section 11J of the Welfare Reform Act 2007";

(e)　in paragraph 21 (treatment of child care charges)–

(i)　in sub-paragraph (11)(c) and (e) after "Employment and Support Allowance Regulations 2008" insert "or the Employment and Support Allowance Regulations 2013";

(ii)　in sub-paragraph (15)–

(aa)　after "paternity leave" in both places where those words occur, insert ", shared parental leave";

(bb)　omit "ordinary";

(cc)　after "maternity allowance under section 35 of that Act" insert ", statutory shared parental pay under section 171ZU or 171ZV of that Act";

(iii)　in sub-paragraph (16)–

(aa)　after "paternity leave" insert ", shared parental leave";

(bb)　omit "ordinary or additional" in both places in which those words occur;

(cc)　after "statutory paternity pay" in both places in which those words occur, insert ", statutory shared parental pay".

11.　In Schedule 7 (applicable amounts: persons who are not pensioners)–

(a)　in column (2) of the Table in paragraph 1 (personal allowances)–

(i)　in sub-paragraph (1) for "£72.40" in each place in which it occurs substitute "£73.10" and for "£57.35" substitute "£57.90";

(ii)　in sub-paragraph (2) for "£72.40" substitute "£73.10";

(iii)　in sub-paragraph (3) for "£113.70" substitute "£114.85";

(b)　in column (2) of the Table in paragraph 3 (personal allowances), for "£66.33" in each place in which it occurs substitute "£66.90";

(c)　in paragraph 4(1)(b) (family premium) for "£17.40" substitute "£17.45";

(d)　in the second column of the Table in Part 4 (amounts of premiums specified in Part 3)–

(i)　in sub-paragraph (1) for "£31.85" and "£45.40" substitute "£32.25" and "£45.95" respectively;

(ii)　in sub-paragraph (2) for "£61.10" in each place in which it occurs substitute "£61.85" and for "£122.20" substitute "£123.70";

(iii)　in sub-paragraph (3) for "£59.50" substitute "£60.06";

(iv)　in sub-paragraph (4) for "£34.20" substitute "£34.60";

(v)　in sub-paragraph (5) for "£24.08", "£15.55" and "£22.35" substitute "£24.43", "£15.75" and "£22.60" respectively;

(e)　in paragraph 18 (the components) after "Employment and Support Allowance Regulations 2008" insert "or regulation 7 of the Employment and Support Allowance Regulations 2013";

(f)　in paragraph 23 (amount of work-related activity component), for "£28.75" substitute "£29.05";

(g)　in paragraph 24 (amount of support component), for "£35.75" substitute "£36.20";

(h)　in paragraph 25(1)(b)(i), after "Employment and Support Allowance (Transitional Provisions, Housing Benefit and Council Tax Benefit) (Existing Awards) (No 2) Regulations 2010" insert "or regulation 26 of the Employment and Support Allowance Regulations 2013";

(i)   in paragraph 27(1)(c), after "Employment and Support Allowance Regulations 2008" insert "or regulation 86 of the Employment and Support Allowance Regulations 2013".

12.   In Schedule 8 (sums disregarded in the calculation of earnings: persons who are not pensioners), in paragraph 12(6)(a), after "Employment and Support Allowance Regulations 2008" insert "or regulation 39(1)(a), (b) or (c) of the Employment and Support Allowance Regulations 2013".

13.   In Schedule 11 (students), in paragraph 3(2)(f), after "Employment and Support Allowance Regulations 2008" insert "or the Employment and Support Allowance Regulations 2013".

Amendments to the Council Tax Reduction Schemes (Default Scheme) (Wales) Regulations 2013

14.   The scheme set out in the Schedule to the Council Tax Reduction Schemes (Default Scheme) (Wales) Regulations 2013(1) is amended in accordance with regulations 15 to 30.

15.–(1)   In paragraph 2(1) (interpretation)–

(a)   for the definition of "contributory employment and support allowance" ("lwfans cyflogaeth a chymorth cyfrannol"), substitute–

"contributory employment and support allowance" ("lwfans cyflogaeth a chymorth cyfrannol") means an allowance under Part 1 of the Welfare Reform Act 2007 as amended by the provisions of Schedule 3 and Part 1 of Schedule 14, to the Welfare Reform Act 2012 that remove references to an income-related allowance, and a contributory allowance under Part 1 of the Welfare Reform Act 2007 as that Part has effect apart from those provisions;";

(b)   in the definition of "paternity leave" ("absenoldeb tadolaeth") omit "ordinary paternity";

(c)   at the appropriate place insert–

"shared parental leave" ("absenoldeb rhiant a rennir") means leave by virtue of section 75E or 75G of the Employment Rights Act 1996;".

16.   In paragraph 10 (remunerative work), in subparagraph (7), after "paternity leave" insert ", shared parental leave".

17.   In paragraph 19(5) (class of person excluded from the scheme: persons treated as not being in Great Britain)–

(a)   in paragraph (j) omit ", an income-based jobseeker's allowance";

(b)   after paragraph (k)–

(i)   omit ".";

(ii)   add–

"; or

(l)   in receipt of an income-based jobseeker's allowance and has a right to reside other than a right to reside falling within subparagraph (4)(a) to (d)."

18.   In paragraph 28 (non-dependant deductions: pensioners and persons who are not pensioners)–

(a)   in sub-paragraph (1)(a) for "£11.30" substitute "£11.75";

(b)   in sub-paragraph (1)(b) for "£3.75" substitute "£3.90";

(c)   in sub-paragraph (2)(a) for "£188.00" substitute "£189.00";

(d)   in sub-paragraph (2)(b) for "£188.00", "£326.00" and "£7.50" substitute "£189.00", "£328.00" and "£7.80" respectively;

(e)   in sub-paragraph (2)(c) for "£326.00", "£406.00" and "£9.45" substitute "£328.00", "£408.00" and "£9.85" respectively;

(f)   in sub-paragraph (8)–

(i)   omit the "or" following paragraph (a);

(ii)   after paragraph (b) insert–

"; or

(c)   who is entitled to an award of universal credit where the award is calculated on the basis that the person does not have any earned income.";

(g)   after paragraph (9) insert–

"(10)   For the purposes of sub-paragraph (8), "earned income" ("incwm a enillir") has the meaning given in regulation 52 of the Universal Credit Regulations 2013."

19.   In paragraph 36 (meaning of "income": pensioners), in sub-paragraph (1)(j)–

(a)   in sub-paragraph (xvi) omit "ordinary";

(b)   after sub-paragraph (xvi) insert–

"(xvia) statutory shared parental pay payable under Part 12ZC of the SSCBA;".

20.   In paragraph 38 (earnings of employed earners: pensioners), after sub-paragraph (1)(j) insert–

"(ja)   statutory shared parental pay payable under Part 12ZC of the SSCBA;".

21.   In paragraph 39 (calculation of net earnings of employed earners: pensioners), in sub-paragraph (2)(d) after "statutory paternity pay" insert ", statutory shared parental pay".

22.   In paragraph 48 (earnings of employed earners: persons who are not pensioners)–

(a)   in sub-paragraph (1)(j) after "statutory paternity pay", insert ", statutory shared parental pay";

(b)   in sub-paragraph (1)(k) after "paternity leave" insert ", shared parental leave".

23.   In paragraph 49 (calculation of net earnings of employed earners: persons who are not pensioners), in sub-paragraph (3)(d)–

(a)   omit "ordinary or additional";

(b)   after "statutory paternity pay" insert ", statutory shared parental pay".

24.   In paragraph 51 (calculation of income other than earnings: persons who are not pensioners) in subparagraph (4), after "Employment and Support Allowance Regulations 2008" insert "or section 11J of the Welfare Reform Act 2007".

25.   In paragraph 55 (treatment of child care charges)–

(a)   in sub-paragraph (11)(e) and (g) after "Employment and Support Allowance Regulations 2008" insert "or the Employment and Support Allowance Regulations 2013";

(b)   in sub-paragraph (15)–

    (i)   after "paternity leave" in both places where those words occur, insert ", shared parental leave";

    (ii)   omit "ordinary";

    (iii)   after "maternity allowance under section 35 of that Act" insert ", statutory shared parental pay under section 171ZU or 171ZV of that Act";

(c)   in sub-paragraph (16)–

    (i)   after "paternity leave" insert ", shared parental leave";

    (ii)   omit "ordinary or additional" in both places where those words occur;

    (iii)   after "statutory paternity pay" in both places where those words occur, insert ", statutory shared parental pay".

26.   In paragraph 72(2)(f), after "Employment and Support Allowance Regulations 2008" insert "or the Employment and Support Allowance Regulations 2013".

27.   In Schedule 2 (applicable amounts: pensioners)

(a)   in column (2) of the Table in paragraph 1 (personal allowances)–

    (i)   in sub-paragraph (1) for "£148.35" and "£165.15" substitute "£151.20" and "£166.05" respectively;

       (ii)   in sub-paragraph (2) for "£226.50" and "£247.20" substitute "£230.85" and "£248.30" respectively;

       (iii) in sub-paragraph (3) for "£226.50" and "£78.15" substitute "£230.85" and "£79.65" respectively;

       (iv) in sub-paragraph (4) for "£247.20" and "£82.05" substitute "£248.30" and "£82.25" respectively;

(b)   in column (2) of the Table in paragraph 2 (child or young person amounts), for "£66.33" in each place where it occurs substitute "£66.90";

(c)   in paragraph 3 (family premium), for "£17.40" substitute "£17.45";

(d)   in the second column of the Table in Part 4 (amounts of premium specified in Part 3)–

       (i)   in sub-paragraph (1) for "£61.10" in each place in which it occurs substitute "£61.85" and for "£122.20" substitute "£123.70";

       (ii)   in sub-paragraph (2) for "£24.08" substitute "£24.43";

       (iii) in sub-paragraph (3) for "£59.50" substitute "£60.06";

       (iv) in sub-paragraph (4) for "£34.20" substitute "£34.60".

28.   In Schedule 3 (applicable amounts: persons who are not pensioners)–

(a)   in column (2) of the Table in paragraph 1 (personal allowances)–

       (i)   in sub-paragraph (1) for "£72.40" in each place in which it occurs substitute "£73.10" and for "£57.35" substitute "£57.90";

       (ii)   in sub-paragraph (2) for "£72.40" substitute "£73.10";

       (iii) in sub-paragraph (3) for "£113.70" substitute "£114.85";

(b)   in column (2) of the Table in paragraph 3 (personal allowances), for "£66.33" in each place in which it occurs substitute "£66.90";

(c)   in paragraph 4(1)(b) (family premium), for "£17.40" substitute "£17.45";

(d)   in the second column of the Table in Part 4 (amounts of premiums specified in Part 3)–

       (i)   in sub-paragraph (1) for "£31.85" and "£45.40" substitute "£32.25" and "£45.95" respectively;

       (ii)   in sub-paragraph (2) for "£61.10" in each place in which it occurs substitute "£61.85" and for "£122.20" substitute "£123.70";

       (iii) in sub-paragraph (3) for "£59.50" substitute "£60.06";

       (iv) in sub-paragraph (4) for "£34.20" substitute "£34.60";

       (v)   in sub-paragraph (5) for "£24.08", "£15.55" and "£22.35" substitute "£24.43", "£15.75" and "£22.60" respectively;

(e)   in paragraph 18(c)(ii) (the components) after "Employment and Support Allowance Regulations 2008" insert "or regulation 7 of the Employment and Support Allowance Regulations 2013";

(f)   in paragraph 23 (amount of work-related activity component), for "£28.75" substitute "£29.05";

(g)   in paragraph 24 (amount of support component), for "£35.75" substitute "£36.20";

(h)   in paragraph 25(1)(b)(i) after "Employment and Support Allowance (Transitional Provisions, Housing Benefit and Council Tax Benefit) (Existing Awards) (No 2) Regulations 2010" insert "or regulation 26 of the Employment and Support Allowance Regulations 2013".

29.   In Schedule 4 (sums disregarded from applicant's earnings: pensioners)–

(a)   in paragraph 5(1)(d)(ii) after "Employment and Support Allowance Regulations 2008" insert "or regulation 7 of the Employment and Support Allowance Regulations 2013";

(b)   in paragraph 6(6)(a), after "Employment and Support Allowance Regulations 2008" insert "or regulation 39(1)(a), (b) or (c) of the Employment and Support Allowance Regulations 2013".

30.   In Schedule 6 (sums disregarded in the calculation of earnings: persons who are not pensioners), in paragraph 12(6)(a) after "Employment and Support Allowance Regulations 2008" insert "or regulation 39(1)(a), (b) or (c) of the Employment and Support Allowance Regulations 2013".

Transitional provision

31.–(1)   The amendments in regulations 6 and 17 do not apply to a person who, on 31 March 2015–

(a)   is liable to pay council tax at a reduced rate by virtue of a council tax reduction scheme; and

(b)   is entitled to an income-based jobseeker's allowance, until the first of the events in paragraph (2) occurs.

(2)   The events are–

(a)   the person makes a new application for a reduction under a council tax reduction scheme; or

(b)   the person ceases to be entitled to income-based jobseeker's allowance.

The Social Security (Information-sharing in relation to Welfare Services etc.) (Amendment) Regulations 2015

(SI 2015 No.46)

Made	*21st January 2015*
Laid before Parliament	*23rd January 2015*
Coming into force	*13th February 2015*

The Secretary of State for Work and Pensions, in exercise of the powers conferred by sections 131(1), (2), (3) and (11) and 133(1) and (2) of the Welfare Reform Act 2012, makes the following Regulations.

Citation and commencement

1.   These Regulations may be cited as the Social Security (Information-sharing in relation to Welfare Services etc.) (Amendment) Regulations 2015 and come into force on 13th February 2015.

Amendments to the Social Security (Information-sharing in relation to Welfare Services etc.) Regulations 2012

2.–(1)   The Social Security (Information-sharing in relation to Welfare Services etc.) Regulations 2012 are amended as follows.

(2)   In regulation 2 (interpretation)–

(a)   for the definition of "social landlord", substitute–

"social landlord" means–

(a)   in a case to which the Housing Benefit Regulations apply, a landlord falling within regulation 13C(5)(a)(i), (ii) or (iii) of those Regulations;

(b)   in a case to which the Housing Benefit (State Pension Credit) Regulations apply, a landlord falling within regulation 13C(5)(a)(i), (ii) or (iii) of those Regulations;

(c)   in a case to which the Universal Credit Regulations 2013 apply, a provider of social housing within the definition given in paragraph 2 of Schedule 4 (housing costs element for renters) to those Regulations;";

(b)   after the definition of "universal credit", insert–

"universal credit claimant" means a person who has made a claim for or has an award of universal credit;

"universal support initiative" means any initiative under which advice, assistance or support is provided by the Secretary of State or any qualifying persons listed in regulation 10(1)(e) to a universal credit claimant for the purposes of assisting them with–

(a)   managing their claim for or award of universal credit, including accessing and using online services, or

(b)   managing their financial affairs.".

(3)   In regulation 5 (supply of relevant information by the Secretary of State)–

(a)   after paragraph (1)(f), insert–

"(g)   where the qualifying person is a social landlord and the relevant information is limited to information referred to in paragraph (3A), determining whether a universal credit claimant, whose award includes or is likely to include a housing costs element in respect of accommodation provided by that social landlord, needs advice, assistance or support in relation to managing their financial affairs;

(h)   where the qualifying person is listed in regulation 10(1)(e) and the Secretary of State or any qualifying person listed in regulation 10(1)(e) determines that a

universal credit claimant needs advice, assistance or support under a universal support initiative–
    (i)   providing such advice, assistance or support to that person; and
    (ii)   monitoring and evaluating the provision of such advice, assistance or support.";

(b)   after paragraph (3), insert–

"(3A)   The information referred to in paragraph (1)(g) is information confirming–
(a)   the identity of the universal credit claimant;
(b)   that the universal credit claimant has a tenancy with the social landlord;
(c)   the date on which the universal credit claimant made a claim for or was awarded universal credit; or
(d)   in a case where universal credit has been awarded to the universal credit claimant–
    (i)   the date on which the next payment of universal credit is due to be paid;
    (ii)   whether the next payment is the first payment under the award; or
    (iii) the amount of housing costs element in the next payment under the award.";

(c)   after paragraph (4)(d), insert–

"(e)   "housing costs element" means an amount in respect of housing costs which is included in an award of universal credit under section 11 of the 2012 Act.".

(4)   After regulation 6(1)(p) (holding purposes), insert–

"(q)   where the qualifying person is listed in regulation 10(1)(e)–
    (i)   providing advice, assistance or support to a universal credit claimant under a universal support initiative; and
    (ii)   monitoring and evaluating the provision of such advice, assistance or support.".

(5)   After regulation 9B (using purposes connected with local welfare provision), insert–

"Using purposes connected with a universal support initiative
9C.–(1)   This regulation applies to relevant information held by a qualifying person listed in regulation 10(1)(e) for the purposes listed in regulation 6(1)(q).
(2)   The purposes set out in paragraph (3) are prescribed–
(a)   under section 131(3)(a) of the 2012 Act as purposes for which the information may be used by that qualifying person; and
(b)   under section 131(3)(b) of the 2012 Act as purposes for use in relation to which the information may be supplied by that qualifying person to another qualifying person.
(3)   The purposes are any purposes connected with–
(a)   providing advice, assistance or support to a universal credit claimant under a universal support initiative; and
(b)   monitoring and evaluating the provision of such advice, assistance or support.
(4)   This regulation permits relevant information to be supplied to another qualifying person only where that other qualifying person is listed in regulation 10(1)(e).".

(6)   In regulation 10 (qualifying persons)–
(a)   in paragraph (1)(a), after "regulations" insert "5(1)(g),";
(b)   after regulation 10(1)(d), insert–

"(e)   for the purposes of regulations 5(1)(h), 6(1)(q), 9C, 16(d) and 17(3)(c)–
    (i)   a person listed in section 131(11)(a), (b) or (c) of the 2012 Act,

> (ii)   a member of the National Association of Citizens Advice Bureaux or the Scottish Association of Citizens Advice Bureaux,
> (iii)   a credit union within section 1 of the Credit Unions Act 1979,
> (iv)   a social landlord,
> (v)   a charity entered in the register of charities maintained under Part 4 of the Charities Act 2011 or a body entered on the register of charities maintained under the Charities and Trustee Investment (Scotland) Act 2005.".

(7)   After regulation 16(c) (holding purposes), insert–

"(d)   where the qualifying person is listed in regulation 10(1)(e)–
> (i)   providing advice, assistance or support to a universal credit claimant under a universal support initiative; and
> (ii)   monitoring and evaluating the provision of such advice, assistance or support.".

(8)   After regulation 17(3)(b) (prescribed purposes relating to a relevant social security benefit), insert–

"(c)   in relation to either of the purposes prescribed in regulation 16(d)–
> (i)   providing advice, assistance or support to a universal credit claimant under a universal support initiative; and
> (ii)   monitoring and evaluating the provision of such advice, assistance or support.".

The Council Tax Reduction (Scotland) Amendment Regulations 2015
(SSI 2015 No.46)

Made	*3rd February 2015*
Laid before the Scottish Parliament	*5th February 2015*
Coming into force	*1st April 2015*

The Scottish Ministers make the following Regulations in exercise of the powers conferred by sections 80 and 113(1) of, and paragraph 1 of Schedule 2 to, the Local Government Finance Act 1992 and all other powers enabling them to do so.

Citation and commencement

1. These Regulations may be cited as the Council Tax Reduction (Scotland) Amendment Regulations 2015 and come into force on 1st April 2015.

Amendment of the Council Tax Reduction (Scotland) Regulations 2012

2. The Council Tax Reduction (Scotland) Regulations 2012 are amended in accordance with regulations 3 to 13.

3. In regulation 2(1) (interpretation), for the definition of "couple" substitute–

"couple" means–
  (a) two people who are married to each other and are members of the same household, but not if the marriage is a polygamous marriage;
  (b) two people who are civil partners of each other and are members of the same household; or
  (c) two people who are neither married to each other nor civil partners of each other but who are living together as if they were married to each other;".

4. Regulation 16 (persons treated as not being in Great Britain) is amended as follows–
  (a) for paragraph (5)(e) substitute–

"(e) a person who has been granted, or who is deemed to have been granted, leave outside the rules made under section 3(2) of the Immigration Act 1971 where that leave is–
  (i) discretionary leave to enter or remain in the United Kingdom;
  (ii) leave to remain under the Destitution Domestic Violence concession; or
  (iii) leave deemed to have been granted by virtue of regulation 3 of the Displaced Persons (Temporary Protection) Regulations 2005;";

  (b) omit "or" after paragraph (5)(f); and
  (c) after paragraph (5)(g) insert–

"".;
  (h) in receipt of income support, an income-based jobseeker's allowance or on an income-related employment and support allowance; or
  (i) a person who is treated as a worker for the purpose of the definition of "qualified person" in regulation 6(1) of the 2006 Regulations pursuant to regulation 5 of the Accession of Croatia (Immigration and Worker Authorisation) Regulations 2013 (right of residence of a Croatian who is an accession State national subject to worker authorisation).".

5. Regulation 19 (persons subject to immigration control) is amended as follows–
  (a) the existing text becomes paragraph (1);
  (b) in that paragraph omit "within the meaning given in section 115(9) of the Immigration and Asylum Act"; and
  (c) after paragraph (1) insert–

"(2)   In paragraph (1) "a person subject to immigration control" has the meaning given in section 115(9) of the Immigration and Asylum Act, but does not include a person who is–

(a)   a national of a state which has ratified the European Convention on Social and Medical Assistance (done in Paris on 11th December 1953) or a state which has ratified the Council of Europe Social Charter (signed in Turin on 18th October 1961); and

(b)   lawfully present in the United Kingdom.".

6.   In regulation 67 (non-dependant deductions)–

(a)   in paragraph (1)–

    (i)   in sub-paragraph (a) for "£11.35" substitute "£11.70"; and

    (ii)   in sub-paragraph (b) for "£3.75" substitute "£3.85"; and

(b)   in paragraph (2)–

    (i)   in sub-paragraph (a) for "£188.00" substitute "£189.00";

    (ii)   in sub-paragraph (b) for–

        (aa)   "£188.00" substitute "£189.00";

        (bb)   "£326.00" substitute "£328.00"; and

        (cc)   "£7.50" substitute "£7.70"; and

    (iii) in sub-paragraph (c) for–

        (aa)   "£326.00" substitute "£328.00";

        (bb)   "£406.00" substitute "£408.00"; and

        (cc)   "£9.50" substitute "£9.80".

(c)   after paragraph (7)(d) insert–

"; or

(e)   the non-dependant is not residing with the applicant because the non-dependant is a member of the regular forces or the reserve forces (within the meaning of section 374 of the Armed Forces Act 2006) who is absent, while on operations, from the dwelling usually occupied as that person's home.".

7.   In regulation 90C(1) (review panel), after "applications" insert "and must also appoint one of the persons to act as senior reviewer".

8.   Regulation 90D (conduct of further reviews) is amended as follows–

(a)   in paragraph (5), for "member of the panel who is undertaking that review" substitute "senior reviewer";

(b)   in paragraph (6)(a), after "review" insert ", having regard to any guidance issued by the senior reviewer";

(c)   omit "and" after paragraph (6)(d);

(d)   after paragraph (6)(e) insert–

"; and

(f)   must give full reasons for the decision to uphold or reject the request for review, if asked to do so by a party to that review within 14 days of the date on which the decision was given."; and

(e)   after paragraph (6) insert–

"(6A)   A member of the panel may set aside a decision disposing of a request for further review if satisfied that it is in the interests of justice to do so.

(6B)   Where a decision is set aside the further review must be undertaken again.

(6C)   A request to set aside a decision must–

(a)   be made within 14 days of the date on which the decision was given, and

(b)   give reasons for the request.".

9.   In Schedule 1 (applicable amount)–

(a)   in the table in paragraph 1 (personal allowances)–

      (i)   in entry (1)(a) and (b) for ''£72.40'' substitute ''£73.10'';

      (ii)   in entry (1)(c) for ''£57.35'' substitute ''£57.90'';

      (iii) in entry (2) for ''£72.40'' substitute ''£73.10''; and

      (iv) in entry (3) for ''£113.70'' substitute ''£114.85'';

  (b)   in the table in paragraph 3 (personal allowances), in entries (a) and (b) for ''£66.33'' substitute ''£66.90'';

  (c)   in the table in paragraph 17 (amounts of disability premiums), in the entry–

      (i)   "Disability premium" for–

          (aa) ''£31.85'' substitute ''£32.25''; and

          (bb) ''£45.40'' substitute ''£45.95'';

      (ii)   "Severe disability premium" for–

          (aa) ''£61.10'' on both occasions where it appears substitute ''£61.85''; and

          (bb) ''£122.20'' substitute ''£123.70'';

      (iii) "Disabled child premium" for ''£59.50'' substitute ''£60.06'';

      (iv) "Carer premium" for ''£34.20'' substitute ''£34.60''; and

      (v)   "Enhanced disability premium" for–

          (aa) ''£24.08'' substitute ''£24.43'';

          (bb) ''£15.55'' substitute ''£15.75''; and

          (cc) ''£22.35'' substitute ''£22.60'';

  (d)   in paragraph 23 (amount of work-related activity component) for ''£28.75'' substitute ''£29.05''; and

  (e)   in paragraph 24 (amount of support component) for ''£35.75'' substitute ''£36.20''.

10.   In Schedule 2 (amount of alternative maximum council tax reduction), in the table in paragraph 1(a)–

  (a)   in entry (b)(i) for ''£185.00'' substitute ''£186.00''; and

  (b)   in entry (b)(ii) for–

      (i)   ''£185.00'' substitute ''£186.00''; and

      (ii)   ''£241.00'' substitute ''£242.00''.

11.   In paragraph 9 (disregard of earnings) of Schedule 3, for sub-paragraph (1)(a) substitute–

"(a)   a part-time fire-fighter employed by the Scottish Fire and Rescue Service established under section 1A of the Fire (Scotland) Act 2005;".

12.   In paragraph 57 (payments to be disregarded) of Schedule 4, for "sections 12A to 12C", substitute "under sections 12A to 12D".

13.   After paragraph 11 of Schedule 5 (capital to be disregarded) insert–

"**11A.**–(1)   The total amount of any payments disregarded under paragraph 18 of Schedule 10 to the Universal Credit Regulations 2013, where the award in respect of which the payments last fell to be disregarded under those Regulations is in existence on the date on which the application for a council tax reduction is made or terminated immediately before that date.

(2)   Any disregard which applies under sub-paragraph (1) has effect until expiry of the period of entitlement to council tax reduction, which period is to be determined in accordance with paragraph 11(3).".

Amendment of the Council Tax Reduction (State Pension Credit) (Scotland) Regulations 2012

14.   The Council Tax Reduction (State Pension Credit) (Scotland) Regulations 2012 are amended in accordance with regulations 15 to 23.

15.   In regulation 2(1) (interpretation), for the definition of "couple", substitute–

''couple'' means–

  (a)   two people who are married to each other and are members of the same household, but not if the marriage is a polygamous marriage;

(b) two people who are civil partners of each other and are members of the same household; or

(c) two people who are neither married to each other nor civil partners of each other but who are living together as if they were married to each other;".

16. Regulation 16 (persons treated as not being in Great Britain) is amended as follows–

(a) for paragraph (5)(e) substitute–

"(e) a person who has been granted, or who is deemed to have been granted, leave outside the rules made under section 3(2) of the Immigration Act 1971 where that leave is–

(i) discretionary leave to enter or remain in the United Kingdom;

(ii) leave to remain under the Destitution Domestic Violence concession; or

(iii) leave deemed to have been granted by virtue of regulation 3 of the Displaced Persons (Temporary Protection) Regulations 2005;";

(b) omit "or" after paragraph (5)(f); and

(c) after paragraph (5)(g) insert–

".;

(h) in receipt of income support, an income-based jobseeker's allowance or on an income-related employment and support allowance; or

(i) a person who is treated as a worker for the purpose of the definition of "qualified person" in regulation 6(1) of the 2006 Regulations pursuant to regulation 5 of the Accession of Croatia (Immigration and Worker Authorisation) Regulations 2013 (right of residence of a Croatian who is an accession State national subject to worker authorisation).".

17. Regulation 19 (persons subject to immigration control) is amended as follows–

(a) the existing text becomes paragraph (1);

(b) in that paragraph omit "within the meaning given in section 115(9) of the Immigration and Asylum Act 1999"; and

(c) after paragraph (1) insert–

"(2) In paragraph (1) "a person subject to immigration control" has the meaning given in section 115(9) of the Immigration and Asylum Act 1999, but does not include a person who–

(a) is a national of a state which has ratified the European Convention on Social and Medical Assistance (done in Paris on 11th December 1953) or a state which has ratified the Council of Europe Social Charter (signed in Turin on 18th October 1961); and

(b) is lawfully present in the United Kingdom.".

18. In regulation 48 (non-dependant deductions)–

(a) in paragraph (1)–

(i) in sub-paragraph (a) for "£11.35" substitute "£11.70"; and

(ii) in sub-paragraph (b) for "£3.75" substitute "£3.85"; and

(b) in paragraph (2)–

(i) in sub-paragraph (a) for "£188.00" substitute "£189.00";

(ii) in sub-paragraph (b) for–

(aa) "£188.00" substitute "£189.00";

(bb) "£326.00" substitute "£328.00"; and

(cc) "£7.50" substitute "£7.70"; and

(iii) in sub-paragraph (c) for–

(aa) "£326.00" substitute "£328.00";

(bb) "£406.00" substitute "£408.00"; and

(cc) "£9.50" substitute "£9.80".
(c) in paragraph (7)–
  (i) omit "or" after sub-paragraph (c); and
  (ii) after sub-paragraph (d) insert–

"; or
(e) the non-dependant is not residing with the applicant because the non-dependant is a member of the regular forces or the reserve forces (within the meaning of section 374 of the Armed Forces Act 2006) who is absent, while on operations, from the dwelling usually occupied as that person's home.".

19. Regulation 70C (conduct of further reviews) is amended as follows–
(a) in paragraph (5), for "member of the panel who is undertaking that review" substitute "senior reviewer appointed under regulation 90C(1) of the Council Tax Reduction Regulations";
(b) in paragraph (6)(a), after "review" insert ", having regard to any guidance issued by the senior reviewer appointed under regulation 90C(1) of the Council Tax Reduction Regulations";
(c) omit "and" after paragraph (6)(d);
(d) after paragraph (6)(e) insert–

"; and
(f) must give full reasons for the decision to uphold or reject the request for review, if asked to do so by a party to that review within 14 days of the date on which the decision was given."; and

(e) after paragraph (6) insert–

"(6A) A member of the panel may set aside a decision disposing of a request for further review if satisfied that it is in the interests of justice to do so.
(6B) Where a decision is set aside the further review must be undertaken again.
(6C) A request to set aside a decision must–
(a) be made within 14 days of the date on which the decision was given, and
(b) give reasons for the request.".

20. In Schedule 1 (applicable amount)–
(a) in the table in paragraph 2 (personal allowances)–
  (i) in entry (1)(a) "£148.35" substitute "£151.20";
  (ii) in entry (1)(b) for "£165.15" substitute "£166.05";
  (iii) in entry (2)(a) for "£226.50" substitute "£230.85";
  (iv) in entry (2)(b) for "£247.20" substitute "£248.30";
  (v) in entry (3)(a) for "£226.50" substitute "£230.85";
  (vi) in entry (3)(b) for "£78.15" substitute "£79.65";
  (vii) in entry (4)(a) for "£247.20" substitute "£248.30"; and
  (viii) in entry (4)(b) for "£82.05" substitute "£82.25";
(b) in the table in paragraph 3 (personal allowances), in entries (a) and (b) for "£66.33" substitute "£66.90"; and
(c) in the table in paragraph 13 (amount of disability premium)–
  (i) in entry (1) (severe disability premium)–
    (aa) for "£61.10" on both occasions where it appears substitute "£61.85"; and
    (bb) for "£122.20" substitute "£123.70";
  (ii) in entry (2) (enhanced disability premium) for "£24.08" substitute "£24.43";
  (iii) in entry (3) (disabled child premium) for "£59.50" substitute "£60.06"; and
  (iv) in entry (4) (carer premium) for "£34.20" substitute "£34.60".

21.   In paragraph 3 (disregard of earnings) of Schedule 2, for sub-paragraph (2)(b) substitute–

"(b)   as a part-time fire-fighter employed by the Scottish Fire and Rescue Service established under section 1A of the Fire (Scotland) Act 2005;".

22.   Schedule 4 (capital disregards) is amended as follows–
(a)   in paragraph 21(2) (benefits to be disregarded)–
    (i)   at the end of sub-paragraph (m) omit "or"; and
    (ii)   after sub-paragraph (n) insert–

"; or
(o)   any social fund payment made pursuant to Part 8 of the 1992 Act.";

(b)   in paragraph 22 (payments to be disregarded)–
    (i)   at the end of sub-paragraph (2)(c) omit "or";
    (ii)   after sub-paragraph (1)(d) insert–

"; or
(e)   paragraph 18 of Schedule 10 to the Universal Credit Regulations 2013,";

    (iii)   in sub-paragraph (4), in the definition of "the relevant date" omit paragraph (a) and, in paragraph (b) the words "in any other case,"; and
(c)   in paragraph 29 (payments to be disregarded), before "sections 12A to 12D", insert "under".

23.   In Schedule 5 (amount of alternative maximum council tax reduction), in the table in paragraph 1(c)–
(a)   in entry (b)(i) for "£185.00" substitute "£186.00"; and
(b)   in entry (b)(ii)–
    (i)   for "£185.00" substitute "£186.00"; and
    (ii)   for "£241.00" substitute "£242.00".

The Social Security (Miscellaneous Amendments) Regulations 2015
(SI 2015 No.67)

Made	*26th January 2015*
Laid before Parliament	*2nd February 2015*
Coming into force	*23rd February 2015*

The Secretary of State for Work and Pensions makes the following Regulations in exercise of the powers conferred by sections 182C(1) and 189(4) of the Social Security Administration Act 1992 ("the Administration Act"), sections 35(3), 35B(11), 136(3) and (5), 136A, 137(1), 138(2) and (4), 175(1), (3) and (4) of the Social Security Contributions and Benefits Act 1992, sections 12(1) and (4), 35(1) and 36(2) and (4) of the Jobseekers Act 1995, sections 15(3) and (6), 17(1) and 19(1) of the State Pension Credit Act 2002, sections 17(1) and (3), 24(1) and 25, (2) and (3) and (5)(a) of the Welfare Reform Act 2007 and sections 8(3), 40 and 42(1), (2) and (3)(a) of, and paragraph 4(1)(b) and (3)(a) of Schedule 1 to, the Welfare Reform Act 2012.

In accordance with section 173(1)(b) of the Administration Act, the Secretary of State has obtained the agreement of the Social Security Advisory Committee that proposals in respect of these Regulations need not be referred to it.

In respect of provisions in these Regulations relating to housing benefit, in accordance with section 176(1) of the Administration Act, the Secretary of State has consulted with organisations appearing to him to be representative of the authorities concerned.

Citation and commencement
1. These Regulations may be cited as the Social Security (Miscellaneous Amendments) Regulations 2015 and come into force on 23rd February 2015.

Service User amendments
2.–(1) Paragraph (2) amends the following provisions–

(a)-(c) *[Omitted]*

(d) regulation 2(5) (interpretation) of the Housing Benefit Regulations 2006;

(e) regulation 2(6) (interpretation) of the Housing Benefit (Persons who have attained the qualifying age for state pension credit) Regulations 2006;

(f)-(i) *[Omitted]*

(2) Each of the provisions specified in paragraph (1) (which define when a claimant is participating as a service user) are amended as follows–

(a) after sub-paragraph (a) insert–

"(ab) a person who is being consulted by or on behalf of–
  (i) the Secretary of State in relation to any of the Secretary of State's functions in the field of social security or child support or under section 2 of the Employment and Training Act 1973; or
  (ii) a body which conducts research or undertakes monitoring for the purpose of planning or improving such functions,
  in their capacity as a person affected or potentially affected by the exercise of those functions or the carer of such a person;"

(b) in sub-paragraph (b) for "sub-paragraph (a)" substitute "sub-paragraphs (a) or (ab)".

(3) *[Omitted]*

Amendment of the Housing Benefit Regulations 2006
6. At the end of regulation 59(4) (calculation of grant income) of the Housing Benefit Regulations 2006 add "or paid under section 63(6) of the Health Services and Public Health Act 1968".

The Social Security (Penalty as Alternative to Prosecution) (Maximum Amount) Order 2015

(SI 2015 No.202)

Made   *10th February 2015*
Coming into force   *1st April 2015*

The Secretary of State for Work and Pensions makes the following Order in exercise of the powers conferred by section 115A(3B)(b) and 189(4) of the Social Security Administration Act 1992.

A draft of this order has been laid before Parliament in accordance with section 190(1) of that Act, and approved by resolution of each House of Parliament.

Citation, commencement, interpretation and application

1.–(1) This Order may be cited as the Social Security (Penalty as Alternative to Prosecution) (Maximum Amount) Order 2015 and comes into force on 1st April 2015.

(2) In this Order "the 1992 Act" means the Social Security Administration Act 1992.

(3) The amendment made by article 2 applies only in relation to an act or omission referred to in paragraph (a) of section 115A(1) of the 1992 Act which appears, to the Secretary of State or the authority mentioned in that subsection, to have occurred wholly on or after 1st April 2015.

Amended amount of maximum penalty

2. In section 115A(3)(b) of the 1992 Act (penalty as alternative to prosecution), for ''£2000'' substitute ''£5000''.

The Social Security (Miscellaneous Amendments No.2) Regulations 2015

(SI 2015 No.478)

Made   *3rd March 2015*
Laid before Parliament   *4th March 2015*
Coming into force in accordance with regulation 1

These Regulations are made by the Treasury and the Commissioners for Her Majesty's Revenue and Customs with the concurrence of the Secretary of State in relation to regulations 14, 17, 21 and 25 and the Department for Social Development in relation to regulations 14, 17, 21 and 26.

The powers exercised by the Treasury are those conferred by sections 1(6) and (7), 2(2)(b) and (2A), 3(2) and (3), 12(6), 13(1) and (7), 19(3) and (5A), 119 and 175(3) and (4) of, and paragraphs 7B, 7BB, and 8(1)(q) and (1A) of Schedule 1 to, the Social Security Contributions and Benefits Act 1992, sections 1(6) and (7), 2(2)(b) and (2A), 3(2) and (3), 12(6), 13(1) and (7), 19(3) and (5A), 119 and 171(3) and (4) of, and paragraphs 7B, 7BB and 8(1)(q) and (1A) of Schedule 1 to, the Social Security Contributions and Benefits (Northern Ireland) Act 1992, and section 3 of the National Insurance Contributions Act 2015 and now exercisable by them.

The powers exercised by the Commissioners for Her Majesty's Revenue and Customs are those conferred by sections 17 and 175(4) of and paragraph 6 of Schedule 1 to, the Social Security Contributions and Benefits Act 1992 and sections 17 and 171(4) of, and paragraph 6 of Schedule 1 to, the Social Security Contributions and Benefits (Northern Ireland) Act 1992 and now exercisable by them.

Citation, commencement and effect

1.–(1) These Regulations may be cited as the Social Security (Miscellaneous Amendments No. 2) Regulations 2015.

(2)-(3) *[Omitted]*

(4) Subject to paragraph (2) of this regulation, these regulations come into force on 6th April 2015.

Amendment of the Housing Benefit Regulations 2006

33.–(1) The Housing Benefit Regulations 2006 are amended as follows.

(2) In regulation 34(c) (disregard of changes in tax, contributions etc) for "small earnings exception" substitute "small profits threshold".

(3) In regulation 39(2)(a) (deduction of tax and contributions of self-employed earners)–

(a) for "11(1)" substitute "11(2)";

(b) for "11(3)" substitute "11(8)"; and

(c) for "small earnings exception" substitute "small profits threshold".

Amendment of the Housing Benefit (Persons who have attained the qualifying age for state pension credit) Regulations 2006

34.–(1) The Housing Benefit (Persons who have attained the qualifying age for state pension credit) Regulations 2006 are amended as follows.

(2) In regulation 34(c) (disregard of changes in tax, contributions etc) for "small earnings exception" substitute "small profits threshold".

(3) In regulation 40(2)(a) (deduction of tax and contributions of self-employed earners)–

(a) for "11(1)" substitute "11(2)";

(b) for "11(3)" substitute "11(8)"; and

(c) for "small earnings exception" substitute "small profits threshold".

The Welfare Reform Act 2012 (Commencement No.23 and Transitional and Transitory Provisions) Order 2015

(SI 2015 No.634)

Made	*10th March 2015*

The Secretary of State for Work and Pensions makes the following Order in exercise of the powers conferred by section 150(3) and (4)(a), (b)(i) and (c) of the Welfare Reform Act 2012:

Citation

1. This Order may be cited as the Welfare Reform Act 2012 (Commencement No. 23 and Transitional and Transitory Provisions) Order 2015.

Interpretation

2.–(1) In this Order–

"the No. 9 Order" means the Welfare Reform Act 2012 (Commencement No. 9 and Transitional and Transitory Provisions and Commencement No. 8 and Savings and Transitional Provisions (Amendment)) Order 2013;

(2)-(5) *[Omitted]*

Transitional provision: claims for housing benefit, income support or a tax credit

7.–(1) Except as provided by paragraphs (2) to (6), a person may not make a claim for housing benefit, income support or a tax credit (in the latter case, whether or not as part of a Tax Credits Act couple) on any date where, if that person made a claim for universal credit on that date (in the capacity, whether as a single person or as part of a couple, in which he or she is permitted to claim universal credit under the Universal Credit Regulations 2013), the provisions of the Act listed in Schedule 2 to the No. 9 Order would come into force under article 3(1) and (2)(a) of this Order in relation to a claim for universal credit.

(2) Paragraph (1) does not apply to a claim for housing benefit, income support or a tax credit where, by virtue of a determination made under regulation 4 of the Universal Credit (Transitional Provisions) Regulations 2014, the person in question would be prevented from making a claim for universal credit as referred to in that paragraph.

(3) Paragraph (1) does not apply to a claim for housing benefit in respect of specified accommodation.

(4) Paragraph (1) does not apply to a claim for housing benefit or a tax credit where–

(a) in the case of a claim for housing benefit, the claim is made by a person who has reached the qualifying age for state pension credit, or by a person who is a member of a State Pension Credit Act couple the other member of which has reached that age;

(b) *[Omitted]*

(5)-(7) *[Omitted]*

(8) Subject to paragraph (9), for the purposes of this article–

(a) a claim for housing benefit, income support or a tax credit is made by a person on the date on which he or she takes any action which results in a decision on a claim being required under the relevant Regulations; and

(b) it is irrelevant that the effect of any provision of the relevant Regulations is that, for the purpose of those Regulations, the claim is made or treated as made on a date that is earlier than the date on which that action is taken.

(9) Where under the provisions referred to in paragraph (10), a claim for housing benefit or income support is treated as made at a date that is earlier than the date on which the action referred to in paragraph (8)(a) is taken, the claim is treated as made on that earlier date.

(10) The provisions referred to are–

(a) in the case of a claim for housing benefit, regulation 83(4E), (4F), (5)(d) or (8) of the 2006 Regulations or, as the case may be, regulation 64(5F), (5G), (6)(d) or (9) of the the 2006 (SPC) Regulations; or

(b) *[Omitted]*

(11) For the purposes of this article–

(a) "couple" (apart from in the expressions "State Pension Credit Act couple" and "Tax Credit Act couple"), has the meaning given in section 39 of the Act;

(b) "housing benefit" means housing benefit under section 130 of the Social Security Contributions and Benefits Act 1992;

(c) "income support" means income support under section 124 of the Social Security Contributions and Benefits Act 1992;

(d) "qualifying age for state pension credit" means the qualifying age referred to in section 1(6) of the State Pension Credit Act 2002;

(e) "the 2006 Regulations" means the Housing Benefit Regulations 2006;

(f) "the 2006 (SPC) Regulations" means the Housing Benefit (Persons who have attained the qualifying age for state pension credit) Regulations 2006;

(g) "the relevant Regulations" means–
  (i) in the case of a claim for housing benefit, the 2006 Regulations or, as the case may be, the 2006 (SPC) Regulations;
  (ii)-(iii) *[Omitted]*

(h) "specified accommodation" means accommodation to which one or more of subparagraphs (2) to (5) of paragraph 3A of Schedule 1 to the Universal Credit Regulations 2013 applies;

(i) "State Pension Credit Act couple" means a couple as defined in section 17 of the State Pension Credit Act 2002;

(j) "tax credit" (including "child tax credit" and "working tax credit") and "tax year" have the same meanings as in the Tax Credits Act 2002;

(k) "Tax Credits Act couple" means a couple as defined in section 3(5A) of the Tax Credits Act 2002.

The Care Act 2014 (Consequential Amendments) (Secondary Legislation) Order 2015

(SI 2015 No.643)

Made   *10th March 2015*
Laid before Parliament   *11th March 2015*
Coming into force in accordance with article 1(2)

The Secretary of State makes this Order in exercise of the powers conferred by sections 123(1) and (2) and 125(7) and (8) of the Care Act 2014.

In accordance with section 123(5) of that Act, the Secretary of State has consulted the Welsh Ministers before making this Order.

Citation, commencement and extent

1.–(1) This Order may be cited as the Care Act 2014 (Consequential Amendments) (Secondary Legislation) Order 2015.

(2) This Order comes into force on the day on which section 1 of the Care Act 2014 comes into force.

(3) An amendment or revocation made by this Order has the same extent as the enactment amended or revoked.

Amendments

2. The Schedule (amendments consequential on the Care Act 2014) has effect.

Savings

4.–(1) Despite the amendments and revocations made by this Order–

(a) any provision that operates in relation to, or by reference to, support or services provided, or payments towards the cost of support or services made, to or in relation to a relevant person, and

(b) anything done under such a provision,

continues to have effect for the purposes of that support or those services or payments.

(2) In paragraph (1)–

(a) "relevant person" means a person to whom or in relation to whom support or services are being provided, or payments towards the cost of support or services are being made, immediately before this Order comes into force;

(b) references to support or services provided include support or services that are not provided, but are or may be required or permitted to be provided before the date on which this Order comes into force;

(c) references to payments made include payments that are not made but are or may be required or permitted to be made before that date.

(3) This article is without prejudice to section 16 of the Interpretation Act 1978 (general savings).

SCHEDULE
Article 2
Amendments consequential on the Care Act 2014

Housing Benefit Regulations 2006

24.–(1) The Housing Benefit Regulations 2006 are amended as follows.

(2) In regulation 52(8)(a) (calculation of tariff income from capital), after "sections 21 to 24 of the National Assistance Act 1948 (provision of accommodation)", insert "or under Part 1 of the Care Act 2014 (care and support)".

(3) In Schedule 5 (sums to be disregarded in the calculation of income other than earnings)–

(a) in paragraph 27, after sub-paragraph (d), insert–

"(dza) the person concerned where the payment is for the provision of accommodation in respect of the meeting of that person's needs under section 18 or 19 of the Care Act 2014 (duty and power to meet needs for care and support);";

(b)   in paragraph 57, after "National Health Service Act 2006 (direct payments for health care)", insert "or under sections 31 to 33 of the Care Act 2014 (direct payments)".

(4)   In Schedule 6 (capital to be disregarded), in paragraph 58, at the end, insert "or under sections 31 to 33 of the Care Act 2014 (direct payments).".

Housing Benefit (Persons who have attained the qualifying age for state pension credit) Regulations 2006

25.–(1)   The Housing Benefit (Persons who have attained the qualifying age for state pension credit) Regulations 2006 are amended as follows.

(2)   In regulation 38(2)(d) (earnings of self-employed earners)–

(a)   in paragraph (ivb), omit "or";

(b)   at the end of paragraph (vi), insert–

"or

(vii)   the person concerned where the payment is for the provision of accommodation in respect of the meeting of that person's needs under section 18 or 19 of the Care Act 2014 (duty and power to meet needs for care and support);".

(3)   In paragraph 26D of Schedule 6 (capital to be disregarded)–

(a)   at the end of sub-paragraph (b), omit "or";

(b)   at the end of sub-paragraph (c), insert–

"or

(d)   as a direct payment under Part 1 of the Care Act 2014 (care and support).".

Council Tax Reduction Schemes (Prescribed Requirements) (England) Regulations 2012

36.–(1)   The Council Tax Reduction Schemes (Prescribed Requirements) (England) Regulations 2012 are amended as follows.

(2)   In Schedule 1 (pensioners matters that must be included in an authority's scheme), in paragraph 8 (non-dependant deductions)–

(a)   in sub-paragraph (6)(a)–

(i)   before "blind" in the first place it occurs, insert "severely sight-impaired or";

(ii)   for "blind" in the second place it occurs, substitute "such";

(b)   for sub-paragraph (11) substitute–

"(11)   An applicant or his partner is severely sight-impaired or blind or treated as such for the purposes of sub-paragraph (6)(a) if the applicant or his partner–

(a)   is blind and in consequence registered in a register compiled by a local authority in Wales under section 29 of the National Assistance Act 1948 (welfare services); or

(b)   is registered as severely sight-impaired in a register kept by a local authority in England under section 77(1) of the Care Act 2014 (registers of sight-impaired adults); or

(c)   in Scotland, has been certified as blind and in consequence he is registered in a register maintained by or on behalf of a council constituted under section 2 of the Local Government (Scotland) Act 1994.";

(c)   in sub-paragraph (12)–

(i)   before "blind" in the first place it occurs, insert "severely sight-impaired or";

(ii)   for "blind" in the second place it occurs, substitute "such".

(3)   In paragraph 21(2)(d)(iii) of Schedule 1 (earnings of self-employers earners), for "pursuant to section 26(3A) of the National Assistance Act 1948" substitute "where the payment is for the provision of accommodation in respect of the meeting of that person's needs under section 18 or 19 of the Care Act 2014 (duty and power to meet needs for care and support).".

(4)   In paragraph 25(13) of Schedule 1 (treatment of child care charges)–

(a)   in paragraph (c), after "section 29 of the National Assistance Act 1948 (welfare services)", insert "or as severely sight-impaired in a register kept under section 77(1) of the Care Act 2014 (registers of sight-impaired adults)";

(b)   in paragraph (d), after "blind" insert "or severely sight-impaired.".

(5)   In paragraph 26 of Schedule 1 (additional condition referred to in paragraph 25(10)(b)(i): disability)–

(a)   in sub-paragraph (1)(a)(vii)–

(i)   after "local authority", insert "in Wales";

(ii)   after "section 29 of the National Assistance Act 1948 (welfare services)", insert "or is registered as severely sight-impaired in a register kept by a local authority in England under section 77(1) of the Care Act 2014 (registers of sight-impaired adults)";

(b)   in sub-paragraph (2)–

(i)   after "blind" in the first place it occurs, insert "or severely sight-impaired";

        (ii)   for "blind" in the second place it occurs, substitute "such".

(6)   In paragraph 6 (severe disability premium) of Schedule 2 (applicable amounts)–

(a)   in sub-paragraph (3)–

        (i)   after "blind" in the first place it occurs, insert "or severely sight-impaired";

        (ii)   for "blind" in the second place it occurs, substitute "such";

(b)   in sub-paragraph (4)–

        (i)   after "blind" in the first place it occurs, insert "or severely sight-impaired";

        (ii)   after "local authority", insert "in Wales";

        (iii)   after "section 29 of the National Assistance Act 1948 (welfare services)", insert "or is registered as severely sight-impaired in a register kept by a local authority in England under section 77(1) of the Care Act 2014 (registers of sight-impaired adults)";

(c)   in sub-paragraph (5)–

        (i)   after "blind" in the first place it occurs, insert "or severely sight-impaired";

        (ii)   for "blind" in the second place it occurs, substitute "such".

(7)   In paragraph 5(1)(b) of Schedule 4 (sums disregarded from applicant's earnings)–

(a)   after "local authority", insert "in Wales";

(b)   after "section 29 of the National Assistance Act 1948", insert "or as severely sight-impaired in a register kept by a local authority in England under section 77(1) of the Care Act 2014 (registers of sight-impaired adults)".

(8)   In paragraph 29 of Schedule 6 (capital disregards)–

(a)   omit "by virtue of regulations made under";

(b)   at the beginning of sub-paragraphs (a), (c), (d) and (e), insert "by virtue of regulations made under";

(c)   at the end of sub-paragraph (d), omit "or";

(d)   at the end of sub-paragraph (e), insert–

"or

(f)   under sections 31 to 33 of the Care Act 2014 (direct payments).".

The Deregulation Act 2015 (Consequential Amendments) Order 2015
(SI 2015 No.971)

Made
Laid before Parliament
Coming into force in accordance with article 1(2)

27th March 2015
27th March 2015

The Secretary of State makes the following order in exercise of the powers conferred by section 112(1), (2) and (5) of the Deregulation Act 2015:

Citation and commencement

1.–(1)   This Order may be cited as the Deregulation Act 2015 (Consequential Amendments) Order 2015.

(2)   The provisions of this Order come into force as follows–

(a)   article 1, article 2 (except insofar as it relates to Parts 1 and 3 of Schedule 2), Schedule 1, Part 2 of Schedule 2 and Schedules 3 to 5 on the 26th May 2015;

(b)-(c) *[Omitted]*

Amendments to secondary legislation

2.   The consequential amendments in Schedules 1 to 5 have effect.

SCHEDULE 3
Article 2
Amendments consequential to the commencement of section 64 of (abolition of office of Chief Executive of Skills Funding) and Schedule 14 (abolition of office of Chief Executive of Skills Funding) to the Deregulation Act 2015

Amendment of the Housing Benefit Regulations 2006

8.–(1) The Housing Benefit Regulations 2006 are amended as follows.

(2)   In regulation 2(1) (interpretation), in paragraph (a) of the definition of "training allowance", omit "the Chief Executive of Skills Funding".

(3)   in regulation 53 (interpretation)–

(a)   in paragraph (d) of the definition of "access funds", omit "or the Chief Executive of Skills Funding";

(b)   in the definition of "full-time course of study"–

 (i)   in paragraph (a), for ", the Chief Executive of Skills Funding" substitute "or under section 100 of the Apprenticeships, Children, Skills and Learning Act 2009";

 (ii)   in paragraph (b), for ", the Chief Executive of Skills Funding" substitute "or under section 100 of the Apprenticeships, Skills, Children and Learning Act 2009";

 (iii)   in paragraph (b)(i)–

  (aa)   omit "under section 14 of the Education Act 2002 or the Chief Executive of Skills Funding";

  (bb)   for "either of those persons" substitute "the Secretary of State".

Amendment of the Housing Benefit (Persons who have attained the qualifying age for state pension credit) Regulations 2006

9.   In regulation 2(1) (interpretation) of the Housing Benefit (Persons who have attained the qualifying age for state pension credit) Regulations 2006, in paragraph (a) of the definition of "training allowance", omit ", the Chief Executive of Skills Funding".

Amendment of the Council Tax Benefit Regulations 2006

10.–(1)   The Council Tax Benefit Regulations 2006 are amended as follows.

(2)   In regulation 2(1) (interpretation), in paragraph (a) of the definition of "training allowance", omit "the Chief Executive of Skills Funding".

(3)   In regulation 43(1) (interpretation)–

(a)   in paragraph (d) of the definition of "access funds", for "the Chief Executive of Skills Funding" substitute "section 100 of the Apprenticeships, Skills, Children and Learning Act 2009";

(b)   in the definition of "full-time course of study"–

 (i)   in paragraph (a), for ", the Chief Executive of Skills Funding" substitute "or under section 100 of the Apprenticeships, Children, Skills and Learning Act 2009";

 (ii)   in paragraph (b), for ", the Chief Executive of Skills Funding" substitute "or under section 100 of the Apprenticeships, Skills, Children and Learning Act 2009";

 (iii)   in paragraph (b)(i)–

(aa)   omit "under section 14 of the Education Act 2002 or the Chief Executive of Skills Funding";

(bb)   for "either of those persons" substitute "the Secretary of State".

Amendment of the Council Tax Benefit (Persons who have attained the qualifying age for state pension credit) Regulations 2006

11.   In regulation 2(1) (interpretation) of the Council Tax Benefit (Persons who have attained the qualifying age for state pension credit) Regulations 2006, in paragraph (a) of the definition of "training allowance", omit "the Chief Executive of Skills Funding".

Amendment of the Council Tax Reduction (Scotland) Regulations 2012

18.–(1)   The Council Tax Reduction (Scotland) Regulations 2012 are amended as follows.

(2)   In regulation 2(1) (interpretation)–

(a)   in paragraphs (a), (d) and (d)(i) in the definition of "full-time course of study", for "the Chief Executive of Skills Funding" in each place it occurs substitute "the Secretary of State";

(b)   in paragraph (a) of the definition of "training allowance", omit ", the Chief Executive of Skills Funding".

(3)   In regulation 52 (interpretation: students), in paragraph (d) of the definition of "access funds", for "the Chief Executive of Skills Funding under section 100 of that Act" substitute "the Secretary of State under section 14 of the Education Act 2002 or section 100 of the Apprenticeships, Skills, Children and Learning Act 2009".

Amendment of the Council Tax Reduction (State Pension Credit) (Scotland) Regulations 2012

19.   In regulation 2(1) (interpretation) of the Council Tax Reduction (State Pension Credit) (Scotland) Regulations 2012, in paragraph (a) of the definition of "training allowance", omit ", the Chief Executive of Skills Funding".

Amendment of the Council Tax Reduction Schemes (Prescribed Requirements) (England) Regulations 2012

23.   In regulation 2(1) (interpretation) of the Council Tax Reduction Schemes (Prescribed Requirements) (England) Regulations 2012, in paragraph (a) of the definition of "training allowance", omit ", the Chief Executive of Skills Funding".

Amendment of the Council Tax Reduction Schemes (Default Scheme) (England) Regulations 2012

24.–(1)   The Schedule to the Council Tax Reduction Schemes (Default Scheme) (England) Regulations 2012 is amended as follows.

(2)   In paragraph 2(1) (interpretation), in paragraph (a) of the definition of "training allowance", omit ", the Chief Executive of Skills Funding".

(3)   In paragraph 73 (interpretation)–

(a)   in paragraph (d) of the definition of "access funds", omit "or the Chief Executive of Skills Funding";

(b)   in the definition of "full-time course of study"–

    (i)   in paragraph (a), for ", the Chief Executive of Skills Funding" substitute "or under section 100 of the Apprenticeships, Skills, Children and Learning Act 2009";

    (ii)   in paragraph (b), for ", the Chief Executive of Skills Funding" substitute "or under section 100 of the Apprenticeships, Skills, Children and Learning Act 2009";

    (iii)   in paragraph (b)(i)–

        (aa)   omit "under section 14 of the Education Act 2002 or the Chief Executive of Skills Funding";

        (bb)   for "either of those persons" substitute "the Secretary of State".

Amendment of the Council Tax Reduction Schemes and Prescribed Requirements (Wales) Regulations 2013

30.–(1)   The English text of the Council Tax Reduction Schemes and Prescribed Requirements (Wales) Regulations 2013 is amended as set out in sub-paragraphs (2) and (3).

(2)   In regulation 2(1) (interpretation), in paragraph (a) of the definition of "training allowance", omit ", the Chief Executive of Skills Funding".

(3)   In paragraph 1(1) (interpretation) of Schedule 11 (students)–

(a)   in paragraph (d) of the definition of "access funds", for "the Chief Executive of Skills Funding" substitute "the Secretary of State";

(b)   in the definition of "full-time course of study"–

    (i)   in paragraph (a), for "the Chief Executive of Skills Funding" substitute "the Secretary of State under section 100 of the Apprenticeship, Skills, Children and Learning Act 2009";

    (ii)   in paragraph (b), for "the Chief Executive of Skills Funding" substitute "the Secretary of State under section 100 of the Apprenticeship, Skills, Children and Learning Act 2009";

    (iii)   in paragraph (b)(i)–

      (aa)   omit "under section 14 of the Education Act 2002 or the Chief Executive of Skills Funding";

      (bb)   for "either of those persons" substitute "the Secretary of State".

(4)   The Welsh text of the Council Tax Reduction Schemes and Prescribed Requirements (Wales) Regulations 2013 is amended as set out in sub-paragraphs (5) and (6).

(5)   In regulation 2(1) (dehongli), in paragraph (a) of the definition of "lwfans hyfforddi" ("training allowance"), omit ", Prif Weithredwr Ariannu Sgiliau".

(6)   In paragraph (1) (dehongli) of Schedule 11 (myfyrwyr)–

(a)   in paragraph (d) of the definition of "cronfeydd mynediad" ("access funds"), for "neu Brif Weithredwr Ariannu Sgiliau" substitute "neu'r Ysgrifennydd Gwladol";

(b)   in the definition of "cwrs astudio amser llawn" ("full-time course of study")–

    (i)   in paragraph (a), for "neu Brif Weithredwr Ariannu Sgiliau" substitute "neu'r Ysgrifennydd Gwladol o dan adran 100 o Ddeddf Prentisiaethau, Sgiliau, Plant a Dysgu 2009";

    (ii)   in paragraph (b), for "neu Brif Weithredwr Ariannu Sgiliau" substitute "neu'r Ysgrifennydd Gwladol o dan adran 100 o Ddeddf Prentisiaethau, Sgiliau, Plant a Dysgu 2009";

    (iii)   in paragraph (b)(i)–

      (aa)   omit "o dan adran 14 o Ddeddf Addysg 2002 neu Brif Weithredwr Ariannu Sgiliau";

      (bb)   for "y naill neu'r llall o'r personau hynny" substitute "yr Ysgrifennydd Gwladol".

Amendment of the Council Tax Reduction Schemes (Default Scheme) (Wales) Regulations 2013

31.–(1)   The English text of the Council Tax Reduction Schemes (Default Scheme) (Wales) Regulations 2013 is amended as follows in sub-paragraphs (2) and (3).

(2)   In paragraph 2(1) (interpretation) of the Schedule, in paragraph (a) of the definition of "training allowance", omit ", the Chief Executive of Skills Funding".

(3)   In paragraph 70(1) (interpretation) of the Schedule–

(a)   in paragraph (d) of the definition of "access funds", for "the Chief Executive of Skills Funding" substitute "the Secretary of State";

(b)   in the definition of "full-time course of study"–

    (i)   in paragraph (a), for "the Chief Executive of Skills Funding" substitute "the Secretary of State under section 100 of the Apprenticeships, Skills, Children and Learning Act 2009";

    (ii)   in paragraph (b), for "the Chief Executive of Skills Funding" substitute "the Secretary of State under section 100 of the Apprenticeships, Skills, Children and Learning Act 2009";

    (iii)   in paragraph (b)(i)–

      (aa)   omit "under section 14 of the Education Act 2002 or the Chief Executive of Skills Funding";

      (bb)   for "either of those bodies" substitute "the Secretary of State".

(4)   The Welsh text of the Council Tax Reduction Schemes (Default Schemes) (Wales) Regulations 2013 is amended as follows in sub-paragraphs (5) and (6).

(5)   In paragraph 2(1) (dehongli) of the Schedule, in paragraph (a) of the definition of "lwfans hyfforddi" ("training allowance"), omit ", Prif Weithredwr Ariannu Sgiliau".

(6)   In paragraph 70(1) (dehongli) of the Schedule–

(a)   in paragraph (d) of the definition of "cronfeydd mynediad" ("access funds"), for "neu Brif Weithredwr Ariannu Sgiliau" substitute "neu'r Ysgrifennydd Gwladol";

(b)   in the definition of "cwrs astudio amser llawn" ("full-time course of study")–

    (i)   in paragraph (a), for "neu Brif Weithredwr Ariannu Sgiliau" substitute "neu'r Ysgrifennydd Gwladol o dan adran 100 o Ddeddf Prentisiaethau, Sgiliau, Plant a Dysgu 2009";

    (ii)   in paragraph (b), for "neu Brif Weithredwr Ariannu Sgiliau" substitute "neu'r Ysgrifennydd Gwladol o dan adran 100 o Ddeddf Prentisiaethau, Sgiliau, Plant a Dysgu 2009";

    (iii)   in paragraph (b)(i)–

      (aa)   omit "o dan adran 14 o Ddeddf Addysg 2002 neu Brif Weithredwr Ariannu Sgiliau";

      (bb)   for "y naill neu'r llall o'r personau hynny" substitute "yr Ysgrifennydd Gwladol".